Acknowledgments

Mickey King—Thank you for the story inspiration, and for time spent answering all my questions!

Steve Gossard, Curator, Circus Collections, Milner Library, Illinois State University, Normal, Illinois—Thank you for sharing your knowledge of the circus and for putting me in touch with Mickey King.

Susan Hartzold, Curator of Collections & Exhibits, McLean County Historical Society—Whether it be historic textiles or fashions or past exhibits, I can always count on you for answers. Thanks so much for your friendly, helpful manner.

In addition, Audra Van Hoorn, Sue Krueger, Angel Shoemaker, Margie Bateman, and my father, Stephen Funk, have been helpful in answering questions and pointing me in the right direction in researching one or more of the books in the American Quilts series. Thank you, ladies. Thank you, Dad.

Dear Reader:

Ida Lou's Story, though fictional, was inspired by the Flying Wards, Eddie and Jennie, and by Mickey King, a star professional aerialist who performed internationally for many years. At seventeen, Eddie and fifteen-year-old Jennie Ward staged their first performance at the Atlanta (Illinois) Fair in 1904. Their salary for the week was fifteen dollars. Eddie passed the hat after each performance, and enthusiastic fair-goers supplemented their earnings considerably. From humble beginnings the brother and sister act rose to fame as the leading double trapeze team in America and the two were at the top of their careers at the time of Jennie's tragic death in 1918. Eddie and his wife, Mayme, went on to perform and to train other aerialists to stardom, Mickey King among them.

Born Marie Florida Gertrude Comeau, Mickey was twelve when she fell five stories from the fire escape outside her family's fifth-story apartment in St. Albans, Vermont. Mickey's father scooped her up off the pile of lathe and plaster and carried her back upstairs where her mother nursed her back to health, as there was no money for a hospital stay. Six months after the fall, on Armistice Day, she took her first steps. Mickey married a lion tamer and enjoyed a lengthy career and much acclaim as a popular female aerialist. A delightful, endearing woman with an ageless wit and wisdom, she exudes tenacity, charm, and ingenuity, the stuff from which stories are carved.

Eddie Ward's Bloomington training barn has passed from the landscape as has the Washington Street YMCA where so many circus acts of those days trained in the winter and put on a show every year for the hometown crowd. But Eddie's residence at 1201 E. Emerson Street endures as the Grand Hotel, a popular Bloomington restaurant where fried chicken is the star attraction.

Circus memorabilia adorns the walls, recalling bygone days when Bloomington was dubbed "The Flying Capital of the World" and the Ward home served as a "hotel" for young aerialists in training.

If you find yourself in Bloomington, Illinois, it's history you can see, my young friends. Enjoy!

Blessings,

Susan E. Kirby

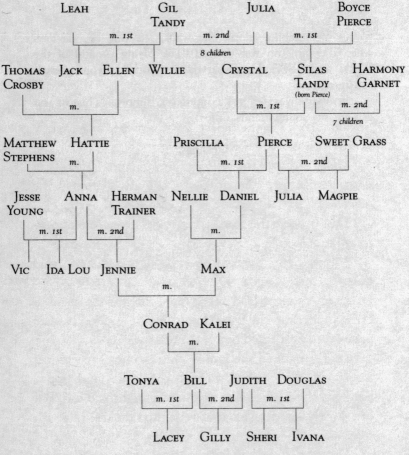

✳ American Quilts ✳

BOOK 4: IDA LOU'S STORY

A L A D D I N   P A P E R B A C K S
NEW YORK   LONDON   TORONTO   SYDNEY   SINGAPORE

To Brandi and Brooke, with love,
And to Bryce Anthony,
Sweet, precious baby

First Aladdin Paperbacks edition May 2001

Text copyright © 2001 by Susan E. Kirby

Aladdin Paperbacks
An imprint of Simon & Schuster
Children's Publishing Division
1230 Avenue of the Americas
New York, NY 10020

Printed and bound in the United States of America

2 4 6 8 10 9 7 5 3 1

Library of Congress Control Number: 2001089058

ISBN: 0-689-80972-7

Prologue

Lacey Tandy raked leaves into a pile. Her stepsisters, Ivana and Sheri, burst out the front door arguing over who was going to hold the new baby first.

"I called it," Sheri shouted, and elbowed past Ivana.

"Too bad. I'm the oldest." Ivana skirted Lacey's pile of leaves and hurried to the minivan.

Lacey dropped the rake and sprinted after them. *But what was the use?* She stopped a few yards short of the driveway.

Dad beeped the horn. "Hurry up, hon. We're running late."

"I'll just stay here with Gram Jennie. Okay?" said Lacey.

Lacey thought Dad might insist she go with them to bring Judith and the baby home. But he nodded instead and waved and eased out of the driveway.

Lacey watched the family minivan until it was lost from view. She scuffed through the leaves and tipped her head back. The sugar maple was bright and full. But one lonely leaf was all that remained on the blue ash tree.

I know just how you feel. Lacey sighed and turned for the house.

For months she had been trying to share in the

excitement of the coming baby. Now he was here. Seven pounds, nine ounces. Scrunched-up eyes and no hair. Or so it seemed from his hospital picture.

Gram Jennie was in the kitchen, loading the dishwasher. She lived in the country. But she was coming to town each day, cooking and helping Dad look after the house and family while Judith was gone. She swung around as Lacey stamped her feet clean. "Lacey! I thought you were going to the hospital."

"I decided to stay with you instead," said Lacey.

The surprise in Gram's blue eyes softened into wordless understanding. She opened her arms and enveloped Lacey in her petal-softness and the sweet scent of face powder.

"Love you, Gram," said Lacey, hugging her neck.

"Love you, too," said Gram. She kissed Lacey's cheek and asked briskly, "How's your quilt coming along? Have you chosen a color for little Gilbert?"

"I was thinking blue. But there's already some blue in the quilt," said Lacey.

"Let's take a look, shall we?" said Gram, letting her go.

Gram was a master quilter, keen on family history and the keeper of the family quilts. With her help, Lacey was making a quilt to honor Tandys both living and dead.

Lacey took her pile of quilt squares from the sewing basket Judith had given her for her birthday. There were sunbonnet girls and overall boys. Each was appliqued to its own white square. Lacey spread the squares over her bed in the order she planned to stitch them together.

"I love the blend of colors. It reminds me of the seasons," said Gram.

"This orange one is for Sheri and the pink is for Ivana. That makes twenty-three," said Lacey. She touched the last completed squares, those she had made to represent her stepsisters.

"One more and you'll have six rows of four across," said Gram. "Nice of little Gilbert to come along and fill that last square for you."

Was it? Lacey wanted to believe so. But making room for a new baby reminded her of the noise and confusion and the difficulty of sharing her father and their little house with Judith and the girls after Dad's remarriage.

"What a precious gift, this child," Gram chatted on. "I can't think of anything sweeter than holding a newborn baby. You'll know what I mean, once you get him in your arms."

"*If* I get him in my arms. I may not, the way Ivana and Sheri are carrying on," said Lacey.

"Cats on a mountain! Is that what's worrying you?" exclaimed Gram. "Why, little Gilbert Union Everett Silas is a Tandy. He'll have enough spunk to get passed around."

Gilbert Union Everett Silas Tandy. They had all written down their favorite name. Dad chose Gilbert for old Gil Tandy, the first Gil on the Tandy tree. Ivana and Sheri chose Union and Everett from their own family trees. Silas was Lacey's pick. Judith was supposed to narrow it down to a final choice. Instead, she put all four names on the birth certificate. "That's too much name," said Lacey.

"Not at all," said Gram. "He'll grow into it."

Lacey shrugged and gathered her quilt squares. She returned them to the basket and skipped a glance from the clock on Sheri's dresser to the window. Her tummy tipped just thinking about the baby.

"Let's go sit in the sunshine while we wait," Gram spoke up. "I have a little mending to do."

Lacey grabbed a book off her nightstand. She followed Gram out to the glider beneath the maple tree. But she was too restless to read.

Gram put on her glasses and spread a patchwork garment over her lap. It was pieced of pinks and purples.

"What's that you're mending?" Lacey asked.

"Ida Lou's first circus costume. See?" Gram plucked a faded photograph from the folds of the costume. Auntie Ida Lou posed before a circus tent. Her hair was in ringlets. There was a saucy tilt to her mouth.

"She had just joined the circus. The other girls in the show gave her scraps left from their costumes," Gram explained. "She crazy-quilted them together and made this. She looks quite pleased with the results, doesn't she?"

Lacey smiled in agreement. She ran her hand over the fabric. It was slick and cool to the touch. It made her think of elephants and clowns and pink lemonade.

"'Baby sister'—that's what Ida Lou always called me, for she was half grown when I came into the world." Gram touched a golden leaf drifting from the tree. She smiled wistfully. "Ida says she was born to fly, and I suppose she was. But it didn't come easily. Not for her, and certainly not for us."

"Us?" echoed Lacey.

"Mama, Poppa, brother Vic, and me. We loved her so. Oh, it was hard to let go." Gram's eyes misted. "Where do I begin?"

Lacey edged closer. Gram pressed her needle into the cloth. With care, she picked a frayed stitch from the garment and a story from her treasure trove of memories.

Chapter One

1918
Bloomington, Illinois
Railroad Town, Aerialist Capital of the World
Pigeons cooed from the sunny shoulders of downtown buildings as Ida Young set out for school. She crossed the street between horse-drawn traffic and chuffing motorcars. A foot-high curbing enclosed the lush green courthouse square. Ida stepped up on it, arms outstretched. Lunch rattled in her tin lard pail as she walked the curbing from one end of the block to the other.

General Useful pulled up to the curb and waved to her from the seat of his wagon.

"Morning, General. Watch this!" Ida pirouetted off the curbing and struck a pose. "Ta-da!"

"Bravo, magirl!" he called, his voice as soft as a breeze moving through winter grass. "Are you off to school? Climb up. We'll give you a lift."

"You're headed the other way."

"Josephine won't mind turning around. She's feeling her oats today," said General.

Ida scrambled aboard his brightly painted dray wagon.

"The elephants are coming," said General.

"Where?" cried Ida, looking both ways.

General's scarred face wouldn't fold into smile wrinkles the way other faces did. But his merry gray eyes gave him away.

"General! You're joking," chided Ida.

"Who, me? Never, magirl!" said General.

In his younger days, General Useful had worked his way up through the circus ranks from candy butcher to lion tamer. He was a scarred patchwork of narrow escapes, with little voice left and nothing outwardly pretty about him. Yet he was almost as dear to Ida as her own runaway daddy.

A block from the school, a group of kids stood in a scraggly line before an old buggy shed.

"What're they looking at?" asked Ida, craning her neck to see.

"I told you, magirl. The elephants are coming. The Wards, too."

"The *Flying* Wards!" Ida clambered down from the wagon and raced ahead. A circus bill covered the whole side of the buggy shed. She swung around and hollered back, "You *weren't* joking, they really *are* coming!"

General winked and tipped his hat and shook the lines over Josephine's back.

Ida gazed at the snarling lions and capering clowns and tumblers and tamers. She closed her eyes and smelled sawdust and peanuts and animals. Heard cracking whips and silvery trumpets and high-stepping horses circling the ring. Gallopy-trot.

The jabbering of schoolmates faded. The street retreated. The nearby church and homes and passing streetcar, too, until it was just Ida and the circus bill. It seemed to her for a moment as if the scene on the buggy shed wall were real and the city were made of paper.

Then the first bell rang with stale offerings of science and sums and fearful news of the war in Europe. Boys and girls crossed the street, heading toward the yawning schoolhouse doors. Still, Ida couldn't pull herself away. "Dizzying, death-defying heights," she read aloud. "Dauntless, daring, intre-intre—"

"Intrepid."

Ida swung around. A slender boy with slicked-down hair had slipped up behind her. He'd missed a clump of yellow hair with the brush. It stood up like a dandelion, just back of his center part. "Intrepid," he said again. "It means fearless."

"I know," said Ida, though she hadn't.

The boy read the circus bill out loud without stumbling over a single word. "Have you got money for a ticket?" he asked.

Ida tipped her chin and didn't answer.

"Me, either," he said. "But we've got a whole month to earn some."

"Together, you mean?" asked Ida, surprised. At her school, boys didn't have much to do with girls except to dip their braids in inkwells or let them be nurses in their trench warfare games.

"Two heads are better than one," said the yellow-haired boy.

"Hands, too," said Ida. "What's your name?"

"Sylvester Baumgart. My friends call me Slick."

"Did your family just move here?"

"My brother got drafted, so I moved in with my Aunt Pliney. My folks are gone," he added.

Gone could mean dead. Or it could mean just that, up and gone. Ida didn't like being asked family questions. So she didn't ask him.

"Who are you?" said Slick.

"Florida Louisa Young. Ida Lou, for short."

"What grade are you in?"

"Fifth. How about you?"

"Sixth." Slick put his hand over his sandy eyebrows and stepped closer. His little finger grazed the top of her head. "You know what? You *are* short."

"So is she." Ida pointed out the dark-haired beauty on the buggy shed wall.

"Jennie Ward? You like her?"

"She's the best."

"What do you know! The Wards are my favorites, too," said Slick. "The men do harder tricks. But girls look prettier coming off a trapeze."

Before Ida could protest, Slick spun around and did handsprings down the walk. He was as quick and light as if he had leaped off the circus bill.

"Do you take tumbling at the Y?" asked Ida, catching up with him.

"Where's that?"

"The YMCA. It's just down the street from our building," said Ida. "I see boys coming and going all the time. Circus people, too. That's where they practice after the season is over and they come home for the winter."

"Do you ever see Eddie Ward?" asked Slick.

"No. Not since he built his own flying barn east of town."

"I'll have to check that out," said Slick. He pecked on her lard pail lunch bucket. "What have you got in here?"

"Hard-boiled eggs. How about you?"

"Biscuits. We could put them together and have an egg sandwich."

"First bell has already rung," said Ida.

"Don't worry. If you're late, just tell your teacher I'm new and you're helping me find my way to class," said Slick. He climbed up on the mounting block in front of the church next to the school and opened his lunch pail.

"But if we eat lunch now, we'll have nothing to eat at noon," said Ida Lou.

"How many eggs do you have?" asked Slick.

"Five," said Ida, taking off the lid to count.

"One now, four later," he reasoned. "You wanna peel it or shall I?"

"I will." Ida scrambled up beside him.

"I figure it'll cost us thirty-five, maybe fifty cents apiece to get into the circus," he said. "Any ideas how we can earn it?"

"I sweep up hair for the barber in our building sometimes. He pays me a nickel," said Ida.

Slick split his biscuit with a pocketknife while she peeled an egg. "You live downtown?" At Ida's nod, he asked, "Do you know all the merchants?"

"Businesspeople, you mean? In our building, I do,"

said Ida, giving him the hard-boiled egg to slice. He ate a bite and put the rest on the sandwich.

"Would any of them hire us?"

"We could ask," said Ida.

"It's settled, then."

"When?" asked Ida.

"How about Saturday? That'll give us a whole day," reasoned Slick.

The last bell rang. Ida crammed her share of sandwich in her mouth and leaped to the ground, spewing crumbs.

But to her surprise, Slick was right about her excuse for being late. It worked.

Chapter Two

June 1918

Ida climbed to the pedestal board and perched on the trapeze. She thrust out her chest and pumped her legs and pointed her toes as she gathered speed. High. Higher! Pushing her body harder. Reaching for the sky. Then she dropped, head down, knees hooked. Just like she used to do on the trapeze bar her father had made for her.

The memory of her father jostled Ida's daydream. Their last family outing before he left had been a circus, followed by a gift, made with his own hands. Ida reached under the bed for the trapeze. It was rusty and too small for her now. But she held it tight, remembering.

"Ida Lou? Shake a leg!" Ida's brother, Vic, hollered from the kitchen.

The pipes creaked as he ran water and splashed and sang as he got ready for work:

"The Yanks are coming! The Yanks are coming!
So prepare! Say a prayer!
The drums rum-tumming everywhere!"

Vic wanted to join the fighting overseas. But Mom needed him at home, and the draft couldn't take him because he was only sixteen. Ida pulled a pillow over her head and tried to slip back into her daydream.

"Are you up? Don't make me come in there!" Vic pounded on the other side of the wall.

Ida covered her eyes as loose plaster sifted over her bed. "Quit, Vic," she hollered. "You're knocking the plaster off the wall!"

"Get up! You've got Saturday chores waiting."

Saturday! Remembering her plans with Slick, Ida rolled out of bed and reached for her dress. She ran a brush through her hair, then padded out to the kitchen where Vic was packing his lunch for his job. He worked at Mr. Beich's candy factory on the west side near the railroad station.

Ida crumbled cold corn bread into a glass of milk, fetched a spoon from the pantry, and sat down. The wall behind the table was covered in circus posters and newspaper features about Bloomington's many circus performers. It was Ida's handiwork. She had put her favorite columns about the Flying Wards at eye level.

"I bet Jennie and Eddie don't walk on plaster sand," said Ida, rubbing the grit off her bare feet.

"You wouldn't, either, if you'd get the broom and sweep."

"You're the one who beat on the wall."

"Get up and I wouldn't have to."

"Grouch. I was going to ask you to be in my flying act. But now I'm going to ask Slick instead." Ida slurped soggy corn bread. "Slick and Fly, the Flying Youngs. That'll be our show name. Fly is for Florida—"

"Louisa Young," said Vic, poking fun in a singsong

voice. "And the headlines will read, 'Slick and Fly Die Young.'"

Ida pretended she didn't hear and went back to reading her circus wall.

Vic donned his cap and tugged her hair, and left for work. He liked his latest job. Ida was glad. It had made her feel bad when she had caught him with his head in his arms the day he had to quit school. It wasn't anybody's fault. Mom was having trouble making ends meet, and Vic was old enough to help. But giving up school had hurt him some. It was the only time Ida had seen Vic cry. No. That wasn't quite true.

Ida crowded out the thought. Three years wasn't forever. Dad might come back. She still prayed every night that he would.

Ida washed the dishes, made the bed, and swept up plaster. The ashes in the cookstove needed emptying. She was on her way down the fire escape with them when her mother stepped out the back door of the building.

"Be careful where you dump those, Ida. I just finished mopping and don't want them blowing in on my floor."

Ida circled to the far side of the war garden that grew on the vacant lot. She emptied the ash bucket and turned back to see Mom sweeping the stoop with the last of the mop water.

"Is it all right if my new friend from school comes today?" she asked as Mom propped the back door open with the mop bucket.

"As long as you play outside."

"We're not playing. We're going to earn money to buy circus tickets," said Ida. "Guess how?"

"Could I guess later? I have to run upstairs a minute." Mom untied the scarf that kept the dust out of her neatly coiled auburn braids. She always wore a scarf when she cleaned. She paused halfway up the fire escape and called back to Ida, "Don't let anyone track in on my wet floor while I'm gone."

"I'll watch," promised Ida.

General's dray wagon was parked in the alley, but he wasn't in it. Ida grabbed a hip strap, pulled herself aboard Josephine, and pretended to be a circus bareback rider doing fork jumps.

Two motorcars turned up the alley. Ida waved to their white-haired landlord, Mr. Summers. She didn't know the man in the second car. They parked at the far end of the building.

"Mom's floor is wet," Ida hollered.

"We'll circle around front," Mr. Summers replied.

"You changed your dress," said Ida when Mom came downstairs again.

"Just my apron," said Mom. "General says Mr. Summers has sold the building. He's expecting the new landlord to stop by today. I didn't want to get caught in a dirty apron with a rag tied over my head."

"Maybe that was him with Mr. Summers."

"Where?" cried Mom, swinging around.

Ida hugged Josephine with her knees and pointed out the motorcars. "I told them the floor was wet, so they—"

"Ida! You didn't!"

"You said don't let anybody track on it."

"I didn't mean Mr. Summers!" Mom picked up her broom, mop, and bucket and hurried inside, mumbling to herself.

Ida balanced on Josephine's broad rump and cheered herself up, pretending to do flips and jump rope with a hoop.

General Useful topped the steps from his basement apartment and caught her at it. "Strike up the band. It's the enchanting Miss Ida Lou on her fire-breathing dragon!" he called in his cornhusk whisper.

"Fire! Good idea! We're jumping through rings of fire!"

"Yesterday, a flier, today afire!"

"I'm generally useful," chirped Ida.

"That and two bits'll get you into the big top. Who's this coming? A friend of yours?"

Ida turned to see Slick waving to her as he loped up the alley. "Slick Baumgart. He moved in from the country to live with his Aunt Pliney."

"Miss Pliney Washington? I've hauled coal for her," said General. "She's kind of old to be taking in a youngster, isn't she?"

"Older than Moses, Slick says. See you later, General." Ida jumped down, kissed Josephine on the nose, and ran to meet Slick.

Chapter Three

Slick's hair was still wet from the comb. His shirt was tucked in, and his boots were shiny. He frowned at her dusty toes. "You have to wear shoes when you ask for work."

"I'll get them. I have to take the ash bucket upstairs, anyway," said Ida.

Slick followed her up. He studied the circus wall while she washed up and braided her hair and put on shoes. "I'm ready."

Slick pulled a cheap watch from his pocket. "Punctuality is important, too, just for the record," he said.

Ida could tell he wanted her to ask him what "punctuality" meant. So she didn't. Nor did she tell him he was getting newsprint fingers, trailing his hands on the walls from the kitchen through the front room. She swung the door wide and motioned him into the dingy corridor ahead of her. "May as well try the fourth floor first. We'll ask Dr. Parker. He's always nice to me."

Dr. Parker, as it turned out, was making house calls. Ida tried the office next to Dr. Parker's.

"Whose office is this?" asked Slick.

"Mr. Buckley's. He does signs in windows. Gold leafing," added Ida, dropping her voice.

"Why are we whispering?"

"Mr. Buckley doesn't want word getting out where he keeps his stuff. He's afraid someone will rob him."

"You mean he's got gold in there?"

"Shh! Little flat sheets of it in booklets," whispered Ida. "I was here with General one time."

"Who is it?" called a voice from inside.

"Ida Lou Young, Mr. Buckley."

The door opened a crack. Two squinty eyes peered out of a whiskery face wedged between the narrow space between door and frame. "What do you want?"

"Remember me? General's friend?"

"Little Ida." Mr. Buckley opened the door wider. "What can I do for you?"

"It's what we can do for *you*, sir," said Slick. "Would you like to have your floors swept? Or your trash emptied?"

"I do my own sweeping, thank you," said Mr. Buckley, and he closed the door.

"Not too friendly, is he?" said Slick.

Ida found it disappointing, too. But then she thought of circus girls in spangles and feathers. She shrugged and said, "There's plenty more to try."

Plenty more turned them down, too. The whole fourth floor, in fact.

"I'm not giving up yet," said Ida. "There's a lady who makes hats on the next floor. A cobbler, too, and a man who sells insurance. Oh! And a tailor."

On their way down, they met Mr. Summers and

his tall, rusty-haired companion. Having tired of the long, polite version, Ida said, "We're for hire."

"Indeed," said Mr. Summers. "May I introduce you to Mr. Trainer? He's your new landlord."

Mr. Trainer had bushy eyebrows, fine tracks creasing the corners of his eyes, and a reddish-brown mustache shaped like the cowcatcher on a train. Ida thought his name fit him.

"Mr. Trainer, this is Ida Lou," Mr. Summers was saying. "She lives upstairs with her brother and her mother, Mrs. Young."

"Upstairs?" said Mr. Trainer. "That's irregular for a business building, isn't it?"

"Mrs. Young is the janitoress. She and the children have nowhere else to live," explained Mr. Summers.

"She's a widow?"

"Er. Something of the kind. The rest of the fifth floor is all warehouse," Mr. Summers said, and cleared his throat. "If you'd like to see the apartment, we can ask Mrs. Young. Or perhaps Ida will do it for us. Ida dear, would you go ask your mother if I could show Mr. Trainer your apartment?"

"That won't be necessary. I'll arrange something at Mrs. Young's convenience," said Mr. Trainer. He bid Ida and Slick good day.

"What happened to your dad?" asked Slick as they continued down the stairs.

"He works for the railroad. He's gone a lot," fibbed Ida. "What about you?"

"My father's dead," said Slick.

"Oh," said Ida, and she quickly changed the subject. "I think we should split up."

"We'll cover more ground that way," agreed Slick. "You start at this end of the hall, and I'll start at the other."

Two lawyers, a doctor, a dentist, and a land speculator later, Ida found Slick waiting for her at the top of the stairs.

"No luck?" she asked. "Me, either."

"This is harder than I thought it would be," said Slick.

"Don't give up yet. Let's see if Mr. Wilson's got some hair to sweep."

The barbershop was right beside the stairs leading down to the ground-floor lobby. Mr. Wilson was coming out as they arrived.

"Hello, Ida Lou. Who's your friend?" he asked.

"This is Slick Baumgart."

"Did you come for a haircut, young man?"

"Not today, sir," said Slick.

"We're trying to earn money for the circus. But nobody has any work for us to do," explained Ida.

"Business has been slow for me this morning, too," said Mr. Wilson. He took a key from his pocket. "I guess I'll go home and have an early lunch."

"Oh," said Ida, disappointed.

"Would you like for us to sweep your floor while you're gone?" offered Slick.

"Now, why didn't I think of that?" said Mr. Wilson, feigning surprise. "Will you wash the mirror, too, and dust off the chair and straighten the shelves?"

"Sure!"

"How does a nickel apiece sound? No shaving corners, now. Shaving's *my* job," joked Mr. Wilson.

Ida grinned. "You can look it over before you pay us."

"That won't be necessary, I trust you. If you finish before I get back, just pay yourselves out of the change drawer. I'll give you an extra key. Lock up when you leave, and slip it under the door."

Chapter Four

Ida opened all the hair tonics and shaving colognes as she dusted the shelf. It smelled like a whole room full of fathers! She shook a little of each scent on a shaving towel.

"What's that smell?" asked Slick, wrinkling his nose.

"This and this and this," said Ida, showing him the bottles. "I made it up."

"Phew!" said Slick.

It *was* a little strong. But Ida didn't admit it made her nose tingle. She dusted the chair and shined the mirror with the scented towel.

Slick sneezed. Ida echoed it.

"Must be all that hair in the air," she said, rubbing her watery eyes. "Are you done sweeping?"

"Just about." Slick used a coal shovel to pick up the pile of hair. "What do I do with it?"

"In there." Ida pointed out a bucket in the corner. "It's pretty full. We'd better take it downstairs and empty it."

"It's starting to rain. I'll just—" Slick shoveled the hair out the open window. "Oops!"

"What?"

"Nothing," he said, retreating from the window.

Ida darted to the window and looked down to see a

man on the sidewalk, shaking hair off his hat. "Slick! You hit him!"

"I didn't mean to," he said quickly.

Below, the man started to brush hair off a lady's back. The startled lady swung around so fast, Ida thought she would whack the man with her folded umbrella. The man pointed up to the window. Hastily, Ida stepped back. But not before she recognized Mr. Trainer's cowcatcher mustache. "Uh-oh. The new landlord."

"Are you done?" asked Slick.

"Yes!"

"Then let's get our money and get out of here!"

Slick pulled the change drawer open, shoved a nickel in his pocket, and flew out the door.

Ida remembered the bucket full of hair. She couldn't take pay before the job was finished. She grabbed the bucket and was about to step into the corridor when footsteps on the stairs stopped her in her tracks. *Mr. Wilson? Or the new landlord?*

Ida dropped the bucket and leaped behind the curtain where the shaving towels and other supplies were kept. She squeezed under the bottom shelf and hugged her knees to her chest.

"Hello? Anyone here?"

Swish, went the curtain. Ida was eye to kneecap with Mr. Trainer. She didn't have to see his face to know it was him. Little pieces of hair clung to his damp trouser creases. She squeezed her eyes shut, afraid to breathe. He cleared his throat. Then, swish. The curtain closed again.

Ida listened so hard, her ears hurt. Had he gone? She was just about to peek when she heard another set of footsteps and a frosty tone Ida knew all too well.

"If you're wanting a haircut, you'll have to come back later."

"I beg your pardon, madam?"

"Mr. Wilson is out to lunch," said Mom. "I don't know how you got in here, but I think you had better leave."

"Who are you?"

"Mrs. Young, the cleaning lady. Are you going to leave, or shall I get the landlord?"

"As of today, I *am* the landlord."

"You are? Oh, dear." Mom's tone lost its starch. "I can explain."

"Let me guess," said Mr. Trainer. "You saw the cash drawer standing open and no barber, and thought you'd surprised a burglar."

"I'm sorry," began Mom.

"You're not the one who should be apologizing," said Mr. Trainer. "Your daughter—"

"My daughter?" interrupted Mom. "What about my daughter?"

"She was here only a moment ago. I was on the sidewalk below when hair came showering out the window."

"Hair clippings?" exclaimed Mom as Ida hunkered low and fought a sneeze. "You think Ida threw hair clippings on you?"

"Madam, it pains me to say so, but there can be no mistake. I looked up and saw her in the window."

"I assure you Ida would not break into Mr. Wilson's shop," said Mom as Ida squeezed her itching nose. "Nor would she throw hair on anyone!"

"Very well, Mrs. Young," said Mr. Trainer. "Let's wait for the barber. Perhaps he can shed some light on this."

"Choo!" sneezed Ida.

Whisk went the curtain. Mom stooped, then drew back as if she'd seen a snake.

"We were cleaning," blurted Ida, crawling out on stiff knees. "Mr. Wilson said we could. The bucket was full, so Slick threw hair out the window."

"Who is Slick?" demanded Mom.

"My friend from school. Remember? I said he was—"

"And I said play outside."

"We weren't playing, we were—"

"Knocking on doors, trying to hire themselves out to everyone in the building," inserted Mr. Trainer. "I regret to say that Mr. Buckley on four complained."

"I-da-Lou!" Mom's face was as red as the stripe on Mr. Wilson's barber pole. "Is this true? Have you been bothering people all through the building?"

"We weren't bothering them. We were job hunting."

"If the merchants are hiring, they'll advertise," said Mom. "Where is this fellow, Slick?"

"He took his nickel and left like Mr. Wilson said we could."

"Did you take a nickel, too?" asked Mom.

"No. I hadn't emptied the hair bucket yet."

"Then you didn't take anything out of the cash drawer?" pressed Mom.

"No, Mom! I didn't. Honest."

"Very well." Turning to Mr. Trainer, Mom said, "I take full responsibility for Ida. And I assure you she won't be knocking on any more doors."

"Thank you, Mrs. Young. By the way, Mr. Summers tells me you live upstairs."

"That's right."

"You're aware this building isn't intended for residential living?"

"I realize that. But Mr. Summers was willing to make an exception."

"Two exceptions, as I understand it. The old gentleman and his wife in the basement?"

"General Useful looks after the mechanical maintenance. Things I could never do," said Mom. "Lizzy helps part-time with the cleaning."

"So Mr. Summers told me. However, it seems to me there must be something available more suited to your needs."

"I can't speak for General and Lizzy. But it would be a hardship for me, having to leave Ida all day," said Mom.

"I can see that," said Mr. Trainer after a brief pause. "I'll give it further study. Now if you'll excuse me." He gave Mom a stiff bow and made his way out.

"Ida Lou!" hissed Mom when they were alone. "My job, the roof over our heads, the very food in our mouths depend on my getting along with that man, and I must say, we're off to a ragged start, thanks to you!"

"Sorry," whispered Ida.

"From now on, stay out of that man's way. Stay off the stairs. Stay out of the corridors!"

"But how can I get upstairs if I don't—"

"Use the fire escape!" said Mom in a voice that invited no argument. "There's no reason for you to be anywhere in this building but our apartment. Is that clear?"

Ida rubbed her stinging eyes and nodded.

"Very well," said Mom. "Go empty the bucket. Then we'll lock up."

"What about my nickel?" asked Ida, edging toward the change drawer.

"You are not to touch that cash drawer. It was foolish of Mr. Wilson to put that kind of temptation before children."

Scorched ears, and no nickel. Ida fought tears all the way down the stairs. Slick was nowhere to be seen. Some friend he'd turned out to be.

Chapter Five

Ida twitched in her starchy Sunday school petticoat. She glanced out the window to see if it was still raining and met Slick Baumgart's green gaze through the glass. He waved. Ida turned in her chair like she hadn't seen him.

"Ida Lou? Can you tell us what it means?"

"What was it again?" said Ida.

"Loosely translated, the verse is, 'As you forgive, so will you be forgiven,'" said Aunt Lizzy. "Would you tell the class what that means?"

Ida cleared her throat and said in her loudest voice, "It means sorry goes both ways. Like, if there's trouble"—she paused and looked straight at the window—"and your friend runs off and leaves you, you can sock him, and then if he's sorry, you can be sorry, too."

A human hug of a woman, Aunt Lizzy Useful crossed the room and put her arm around Ida. "Ida, dear? Why are you shouting?"

"So Slick will hear me. He's looking in the window," Ida whispered back.

Aunt Lizzy crossed to the window on her heavy gait and slid it open. "Hello, Slick. I'm Mrs. Useful. There's a chair free beside Ida. Join us, won't you?"

Slick crawled through the window and took off his

cap. His dandelion sprig sprang up at center part as he perched on the offered chair.

Aunt Lizzy resumed her lesson on forgiveness. She wasn't really Ida's aunt, she was her Sunday school teacher. With no children of her own, Aunt Lizzy's generous mothering heart embraced every child who had ever been in her class. They all called her Aunt Lizzy, even some of the grown-ups.

Slick nudged Ida. But she didn't look his way or speak. Not for the whole class period. Not even when the closing prayer was finished, and everybody but Aunt Lizzy left.

"How come you're mad at me?" asked Slick.

"You threw hair on Mr. Trainer, and I got in trouble for it," said Ida hotly. "Mom wouldn't even let me take my pay."

"I'm sorry," said Slick

"What good's that do?"

"Ida Lou," murmured Aunt Lizzy.

"Yes?"

Instead of answering, Aunt Lizzy patted Slick's shoulder. "I enjoyed having you in class, Slick. You're welcome to stay for church."

Slick looked at Ida, as if he'd like an invitation from her, too. Ida didn't give him one. "Maybe another time," he said.

"I hope so," said Aunt Lizzy. She smiled and gathered her papers. "I hear the prelude. Are you ready, Ida?"

"Tell Mom I'll be right there."

"If sorry's not good enough, how about if I tell you a

secret?" said Slick when they were alone. "Would we be friends again, then?"

Curious, Ida said, "That depends. What's the secret?"

"I lied to you," said Slick. "My dad isn't really dead."

"So? I fibbed to you, too," said Ida.

"About your dad? Why? Is he in jail?"

"Jail?" echoed Ida. "Well, no!"

"Then where is he?"

"I'm not telling."

"Then I'm not telling you, either," said Slick.

Ida had a feeling he already had. Jail. It was a shock. She had never known anyone with criminals in the family. "What'd he do?" she blurted.

"Nothing. He didn't do anything."

"Then why is he in jail?"

"I said one secret," said Slick. "That would be two. Are we friends again?"

"Will you teach me how to do handsprings?" asked Ida.

"I can teach. The question is, can you learn?"

"Smarty," said Ida.

Slick smoothed down his hair and followed her upstairs.

"If you're staying, you'd better sit still or Mom'll pinch you," warned Ida in a whisper, and kind of hoped Mom would.

Slick stayed for church and went home with them afterward, even though Mom hadn't invited him, and neither had Ida. After a lunch of fried mush and green onions, he went out on the vacant lot to play baseball with Vic and some older boys. Ida wanted to play, too, but Vic wouldn't let her.

So she went to General and Aunt Lizzy's apartment with Mom instead. The sun had come out, and Aunt Lizzy had the door propped open to let in more light.

"Am I late?" asked Mom, joining Aunt Lizzy at the quilting frame.

"Not at all. I'm just getting started," said Aunt Lizzy. "Ida! I'm so glad you're here to help."

Aunt Lizzy's warm welcome was soothing after Vic's rejection. Ida plunked down on General's circus trunk and wondered, as she always did, what was inside. She'd asked General lots of times. He made jokes, dodging her questions. Finally, Mom got cross and warned her at home not to ask anymore, that it wasn't polite to be nosy.

"Thread one for me, too," said General as Ida threaded herself a needle.

"I don't know where you found a quilting man, Lizzy, but he's a fair stitch," said Mom.

"By necessity, madear. A trouper who can't seam his tights is at the mercy of the showgirls."

"A real hardship, I'm sure," said Aunt Lizzy.

The quilt, pieced from scrap fabrics, paraded colored stars on muslin blocks. It was called Ohio Star. Ida counted forty-five star blocks in all. Black-and-white polka-dot sashing strips and red sashing squares set off each block like a picture frame. "Can we keep it?" she asked.

"Don't be silly, it's for the war effort," said Mom, for the quilt was to be Mom and Aunt Lizzy's contribution to the Red Cross Liberty Auction.

"I'll make myself one, then," said Ida.

"You could, with a little help," said Aunt Lizzy.

"Absolutely," agreed Mama. "I learned from my mother and Aunt Harmony. They quilted by the hour when I was small. Then Poppa moved us to Oklahoma for the land run. I sure missed Aunt Harmony. She and Mama would swap scraps of cloth by mail and sew them into their quilts."

"A tangible way of staying in touch," said Aunt Lizzy.

"Exactly," said Mom, nodding. "They remained close over the years. I remember how much it meant to Mama when Aunt Harmony bequeathed quilts to her. My favorite was a crazy-quilt lap throw she had made for Uncle Silas when he fell ill. It was a gorgeous thing."

Though it had been a while, Ida remembered Gram Hattie coming by train once from her home in Oklahoma and staying a few weeks. Ida fingered a pieced star and asked, "Is a crazy quilt as pretty as this?"

"This one was. It was made of rich dress fabrics," said Mom. "Another favorite of mine was an Underground Railroad pattern. Aunt Harmony and Mama worked together on that one. Mama knew I was partial to it, and passed it along for you and Vic. Remember, Ida?

"Perhaps not. Your father took it," continued Mom in her good-riddance voice, the one she saved just for

Dad. To General and Aunt Lizzy, she explained, "Jess worked for the Chicago & Alton shops as a carpenter. Before the war, when there were minor repairs to be done on passenger coaches, he would work while the train was en route."

"It saved them taking it out of service, I suppose," said General.

"Exactly," said Mom. "Jess liked to catch a few winks in the baggage car. He never was all that work brittle. Though why he took the quilt when he knew he wasn't coming back is beyond me."

"Perhaps it helped him to have something that had covered his children," said Aunt Lizzy kindly. She patted Ida's hand, adding, "Little Ida sunshine."

"I hate trains," said Ida.

"How can you hate trains?" said Mom, surprised. "I've always loved them. Even when I was small. My cousin Daniel and I liked to line up Aunt Harmony's dining room chairs and pretend we were going on a train trip."

"Trains took your dad away, too," Ida reminded her mother.

"Poppa got a job as a Harvey cook when our little Oklahoma farm went bust," Mom explained to Aunt Lizzy and General. "Poppa's middle name was Seymour, but my sisters would joke that we saw a lot less of Seymour once he started cooking on trains."

"Trains are trouble," said Ida, puzzled that her mom's sisters could joke about Grandpa's job taking him away from them.

"Nonsense! Trains aren't the problem. Quitters are," replied Mom.

"Speaking of problems, Anna," drawled General, "what's this I hear about you chasing the new landlord out of the barbershop with a mop?"

"That's nothing. A lady on the sidewalk nearly hit him with an umbrella," said Ida.

"Whatever for?" cried Aunt Lizzy.

"Because he was brushing her off on account of the hair Slick tossed out the window," said Ida. "I don't think they'd been introduced, though. She got mad as a wet cat."

"Sounds like a hairy moment, magirl."

Laughter washed over the sound of whispering threads.

Mom patted the quilt top looking for the scissors. "Maybe I'll start carrying an umbrella myself. If Mr. Trainer decides to evict us, it may come in—" She stopped short.

Ida turned to see Mr. Trainer standing on the other side of the threshold, a basket over his arm. His knock on the open door shattered the sudden, taut, pin-drop silence.

"Mr. Trainer!" cried Aunt Lizzy, the first to recover. "Won't you come in?"

"Don't get up. What I have to say won't take but a minute," said Mr. Trainer. He took off his hat and looked right at Mom. "Regarding the subject of eviction, I've decided that if my business tenants aren't inconvenienced by your living here, I have no objections for the time being. However, if there are complaints from other tenants, I'll be forced to ask you to make other arrangements."

"That seems fair," said Aunt Lizzy in her warm way.

"More than," agreed General. He shook Mr. Trainer's hand and thanked him.

Mom thanked him, too, though her face was as red as the sashing squares of the quilt. Ida noticed she didn't hold his gaze for more than a second or two before picking up her needle and ducking her head.

"Perhaps you folks would help me out and take these off my hands," said Mr. Trainer.

"Eggs!" exclaimed Aunt Lizzy, accepting the basket he offered. "Nice big ones, too. How much are they, Mr. Trainer?"

"I'm not selling them, I'm giving them away," he said quickly. "I keep a few chickens in my carriage house. They've turned out to be good layers. Please, I'd consider it a favor," he added, urging the egg basket upon Aunt Lizzy.

"How very kind!"

"No, you'd be doing the kindness," he replied. "A man can only eat so many eggs."

"You live alone, Mr. Trainer?" asked General.

"Yes, at Franklin Park," he replied.

Ida loved eggs. She jumped up and helped Aunt Lizzy empty them into a bowl.

"Thank you again, Mr. Trainer," said Aunt Lizzy, returning the wire basket. "We'll enjoy the eggs. Won't we, Anna?"

Mom looked up from her quilting and blinked as if she'd pricked herself.

"You *did* intend me to share them, didn't you, Mr. Trainer?" Aunt Lizzy filled the awkward moment with her rosy smile.

"Yes, of course," said Mr. Trainer. He flushed and turned his hat in his hand as Mom thanked him.

"What a pleasant fellow," said Aunt Lizzy a short while later, when Mr. Trainer had gone. "And here we were afraid he was going to turn us out!"

"Home sweet home," said General.

"And egg salad, too," added Ida.

Mom murmured, "Perhaps I was hasty in my opinion of him."

"Does this mean I can use the stairs?" asked Ida.

"You may," said Mom. "As long as they're attached to the fire escape."

Disappointed, Ida put down her quilting needle.

"Where are you going?"

"Over to the school to play on the trapeze," said Ida.

But she went upstairs first and sneaked a pair of Vic's trousers.

Chapter Six

Ida swung standing up. She swung sitting down. She hung by her arms, by her knees, by her toes. She soared and dipped and dived, pivoting on and off the fly bar in circus togs that glimmered like fireflies.

Then Ida looked down and saw she wasn't alone. Eddie Ward of the Flying Wards was standing below, his head tipped back. "What do you think you're doin'?" he would say.

"I want to join out!" ("Join up" sounded better to Ida, but she'd say "join out" because that was how General said it.)

"Can you catch?" Eddie would call back.

"I can learn. You train new acts, don't you?"

"That's right, kid."

"I want to fly. Train me !"

And Eddie would say . . .

"Ida Lou, have you been wearing my britches?"

It wasn't Eddie Ward. It was Vic barging into her room with a pair of dusty trousers in his hand. "You have, haven't you?"

"Slick's taking tumbling lessons at the Y," Ida eased into her explanation.

"So?"

"He's showing me what he's learned. They're pretty

slick tricks." Ida wiggled her eyebrows. "Slick tricks. Get it, Vic?"

"Wash 'em in time for the community sing tonight, or you can forget about going with me!" Vic flung the trousers down. Plaster trickled from the ceiling as he slammed her door on his way out.

One night each month, folks gathered to sing and show support for the American "doughboys." Vic was Ida's best chance at going. Still, there were harder things to miss. Like the circus. It had been a month since the posters went up. The show was coming in two days. Slick had money. He was mysterious as to how he had earned it and was making no offers to share. Not that Ida expected him to. She was willing and eager to earn her own way. If only she knew how.

Ida turned the problem over in her mind as she pulled a dress over her shift. She brushed and braided her hair and went into the kitchen. "I'll wash 'em and have 'em ready."

"That's more like it," said Vic, lacing his boots.

"Vic? About the circus. I was wondering . . ."

"Still no money?" asked Vic.

"I can't go downstairs and sweep hair, and I don't know who else to ask," said Ida, pouring herself a glass of milk.

"What's Mom say?"

"'We'll see,'" Ida repeated Mom's exact words. They *both* knew what that meant.

"I'd help you out, Ida. Honest, I would. But I'm broke until payday."

Ida drizzled honey over a liberty biscuit and turned a longing gaze on her circus wall.

"Guess you'll have to settle for the street parade," reasoned Vic. "We can see the train unload, too, if you want."

"Can we go real early?"

"If you can get up, we can," said Vic.

"I can! One call, and I'll jump right up!"

Sometimes, if a circus was shorthanded, they'd hire kids for odd jobs, like carrying water or marching around town, draped in a sign, advertising the circus. Payment was a free pass to the show. At this late date, it was Ida's last hope.

She washed Vic's trousers, hung them over the fire escape railing, and poked a couple of hard-boiled eggs in her apron pocket before carrying the ash bucket downstairs.

Josephine was harnessed to the wagon and stirring flies with her tail. Ida emptied the ashes and plucked grass and clover for Josephine. She tossed handfuls of it into the bucket.

"Here's a treat for you, Josephine!" Ida held the bucket, watching for General. When he wasn't fixing broken things in the building, he hired out himself and his wagon for general hauling, including messes, such as the lathe and plaster pile Mr. Trainer's carpenters were making. They had been hard at work the past month, remodeling the building.

"Ida, magirl! You're up bright and early."

"General! I was waiting for you." Ida raced to meet

him as he climbed the stairs from his apartment. "Are you hauling away plaster?"

"I sure am."

"Can I help?"

"It's heavy work for a lightweight. But you can break the lathes into kindling for Lizzy's cookstove. You'll have to pull the nails first. Where's your shoes?"

"Upstairs."

"Well, get 'em, magirl. I knew a horse once stepped on a nail and caught lockjaw. Locked him up so tight, they had to bury him standing up."

"General! Horses don't get lockjaw!"

"Don't they? It must have been bad oats."

Ida giggled and raced upstairs to get her shoes.

Most of the plaster had separated from the lathes as it was pulled from the wall and discarded. The nails pried loose from the thin strips easily enough. Ida broke the lathes across her knee and piled them by the basement window where Aunt Lizzy could reach them without even having to go outside.

By the time the wagon was loaded and General was ready to go, they were both white with plaster dust.

"Can I ride to the dump with you?" asked Ida.

"Run and ask your mother, magirl."

Ida grabbed the empty ash bucket and let herself in through the back lobby. Her mother had the front door propped open and was sweeping the sidewalk in front of the building.

"I'm helping General haul away plaster," Ida told

her. "We're going to the dump, all right?"

"It's nice of you to help General, Ida. But if he offers to pay you, you aren't to take it," Mom warned. "He and Lizzy have done so much for us, there's no way we could ever repay them."

It was true. Aunt Lizzy was always cooking something for them. And everything that broke, General fixed. He'd bought all the garden seeds for the war garden they were sharing. And when they needed coal or wood for the cookstove, he hauled it home for them.

"I'm just being neighborly," said Ida.

"That's my girl," said Mom. "Take the bucket upstairs first, all right?"

Ida nodded. But she hated circling all the way around the building to take the fire escape up. She waited until Mom turned her back, then darted inside and up the interior stairs.

The corridors rang with hammers and saws and carpenters' voices.

Ida slipped hurriedly along, bucket swinging from her left hand. She ducked past the freshly clipped mayor on his way out of the barbershop, then took the third flight in twos. A long shadow fell over her path as she neared the top step.

Ida grabbed the railing to keep from plowing into Mr. Trainer. The bucket clattered against the wall. Chips of plaster rained on her dusty shoes.

"Look there, you've gouged the wall," said Mr. Trainer, reaching for the bucket.

Startled, Ida let go too fast and dropped the bucket.

"Didn't your mother tell you to stay off the stairs?" scolded Mr. Trainer as the bucket bounced down the stairs.

Ida ducked her head and stared at her dusty white shoes.

"This is no place for children," said Mr. Trainer. "You're liable to get run over by carpenters."

"General's waiting, and this way was closer," mumbled Ida.

"Take the long way, like your mother told you."

Ida turned and started down again.

"Wait a minute!" ordered Mr. Trainer. "Wait right there while I get a broom. You can sweep up the plaster you knocked loose."

As the moments ticked past and he didn't return, Ida fidgeted. What if General got tired of waiting and left without her? She counted to twenty. Fifty. One hundred. No sign of Mr. Trainer. Tired of waiting, Ida raced to the landing, grabbed the empty bucket, and shot down the stairs. Mom wasn't in the lobby. Ida slipped through and out the back door. She flung the bucket under the fire escape and scrambled up on the wagon seat beside General, panting, "I'm ready! Let's go!"

Chapter Seven

The dump was at the edge of town. Tall shoots of grass and thriving weeds grew over clumps of discarded junk. As General stopped the wagon, Ida spotted a familiar face a dozen yards away. "Hey, Slick!" she hollered.

"Ida! What're you doing here?" Slick called back.

"Helping General. How about you?"

"This and that." Slick wiped his hands on the seat of his patched trousers. "What'd you bring to eat?"

"Nothing," fibbed Ida.

"No eggs?"

"Nope."

"Shucks," he said, turning away.

"What's the count on that boy now?" asked General.

"Seventeen hard-boiled eggs," said Ida. She had been keeping track.

"I meant the number of times you and him have fallen in and out of friendship."

"Oh," said Ida. Her cheeks got warm. "It's not my fault. He's always hungry, and he uses big words he knows I don't know, and he's tricky."

"A sometimes-friend," said General.

It fit. Though there was one thing Slick was good at, and that was apologizing. He ought to be, he'd had lots of practice.

"He does seem to have an appetite for eggs," said General, setting the brake. "Maybe Mr. Trainer ought to set him up with his own hen."

"Wouldn't do any good, he'd just eat it," said Ida.

General chuckled and jumped to the ground. Ida climbed down the wheel beside him and offered to help him unload.

"There's only one shovel, magirl. Go see what your friend's up to. I'll let out a whistle when I'm ready to go."

Dragonflies hovered over wet, weedy mounds of debris. Ida scattered them as she ran past. Her shoes wheezed plaster dust as she leaped over a pile of trash and landed beside Slick. He glanced up at her, then went on poking through the debris with a stick. Something rang hollow.

"What's that?" asked Ida.

"A milk bottle." Slick shook out rainwater and put the bottle in a musty-looking crate.

"What're you saving it for?"

"I'm going to clean it up and sell it."

His words rang in Ida's head like two quarters clinking together. "To who?"

"The dairy."

"Snow and Palmer? How much?" asked Ida.

"A penny or two." Slick picked up his stick and prodded something glassy-looking out of the ground. It turned out to be a marble. He pocketed it. "Are you going to the community sing tonight?"

Ida nodded, her thoughts on making money. "Show me what to look for, and I'll help."

"Cut you in, you mean?" said Slick. "Last time we were partners, you ended up mad at me."

"That was different," said Ida. "Mom won't care about this."

"I don't know," he hedged. "I don't like you being mad at me. And besides, this is how I pay for my tumbling lessons."

"Smarty," sniffed Ida, envious of those lessons he was taking at the Y.

"I'm not being a smarty, I'm just telling you I've got expenses. What's that you're kicking at? Move your foot."

It was a gunnysack. Ida picked it up before Slick could.

"Any holes?" he asked. "Let me see."

"Hold on!" Ida twisted out of reach. She held the sack aloft, pinched between two fingers. "No holes that I can see. What's it worth?"

"A penny."

"Good. If I find enough of them, I can get into the circus."

"You won't make it in gunnysacks." Slick's gaze slid to the sack again. "Mostly what you find is worn-out rotten ones. Don't get in a hurry reaching inside," he added. "You're liable to shake hands with a snake."

Ida dropped it quick, then jumped at the sound of something rustling behind her. A dog trotted out of the weeds. He was the size of a beagle, but the color of cinnamon. He wagged his crooked tail and licked

Ida's shoes. "Nice doggie." Ida stooped to stroke his ears.

Slick dived for her gunnysack.

"Hey!" she squealed. "That's mine!"

"You dropped it."

"To pet the dog!" Ida tried to jerk the sack out of his hands. "Let go!"

"It's mine now. *You* let go!"

"*You!*"

"*You!*"

The dog got in the middle of the tug-of-war. He put his muddy paws on Ida's dress and sniffed her pocket.

"Shoo! Get!" Ida tried to nudge the dog away with her knee. "Call off your dog, Slick!"

Slick jerked the gunnysack out of her hand while she was fending off the dog. He shoved it up under his shirt, accusing, "You do too have eggs, Ida. You lied to me."

"You stole my gunnysack!"

"You dropped it!"

"Dad-gum it, Slick," Ida cried. "See why we have trouble?"

"I'm teaching you, is all. And for a penny sack. That's cheap education."

"A *cheat* education, you mean. And you're the cheat!"

"I am not!"

"Are, too."

"For crying out loud, Ida. Take it, then. Go on, take it, if you're going to be that way."

"Fair is fair." Ida took the sack and stuck her chin

in the air, just daring him to deny it.

Slick's gaze fell to her pocket. "Are you going to share your eggs or not?"

Ida rolled her eyes. "You can have one, I guess. But then we're going to work together and no more tricks. Okay?"

"Okay," said Slick, hand outstretched.

"You promise?"

"I said *okay*." Slick peeled off the shell and poked the whole egg in his mouth.

The dog licked his slobbery chops and whined.

"If I had a dog, I'd treat him better," muttered Ida. She broke her egg in half and shared it with the dog. "What happened to his tail?"

"He broke it, wagging," said Slick.

"He did not! What happened, really?"

"Never mind Wags. We've got work to do," said Slick. "You go east, I'll go west. If you see anything that looks hopeful, yell."

Ida stirred through a lot of worthless broken bottles and rusty tin cans before finding a big medicine bottle. It was dirty, but unbroken.

"That's a nice one," said Slick when she showed him. "I can get three cents for that one."

"*I* can, don't you mean?" said Ida. She went back to looking through junk. The dog trotted along at her side and barked as if he saw something she hadn't. It turned out to be a bone.

General let loose a whistle and beckoned to her from the wagon.

"General's ready to go," Ida called to Slick. "Who do I see to get my money?"

"I can redeem if for you when I take my stuff in, if you want," offered Slick, striding to meet her.

"Redeem?" echoed Ida, unsure of his meaning.

"Collect the pay for it," he said. "You said you were coming to the sing tonight. I'll bring your share with me."

"Not so fast," said Ida. "How do I know I can trust you?"

Slick looked hurt. But Ida wasn't going to get tricked again. "Give me something to hold until I get my money."

"Like what?"

"What have you got in your pockets?"

Slick turned them inside out. A bent fork, the marble, and some wooden matches fell to the ground.

"That's all?"

Slick squinted and tapped his foot. All at once he snapped his fingers and called the dog to his side.

"Wags? Your *dog*?" said Ida.

"If you need collateral, he'll have to do. He's all I've got. But just until tonight, when I bring the money. You'll give him some water when you get home, won't you?" he added, misgivings creeping in.

"I shared my egg with him, didn't I?" said Ida. "That's more'n he got from you!"

Slick relieved her of the gunnysack and bottle, then patted Wags on the head. "See you later, boy." He picked up his crate, moved away a few yards, and turned back to wave. "The school, at seven."

Chapter Eight

General Useful had no objection to Wags riding in the wagon with them. Nor did Josephine seem to mind having a dog for a passenger. But when Ida got home, she was careful to be sure Mom wasn't around before starting upstairs. At the second landing, Wags balked and whined and refused to follow her any farther.

"Scairty-cat." Ida picked him up. He was heavier than he looked. She stopped on the landings between floors to rest, and still, her arms were about to break by the time she reached their apartment.

Wags explored the kitchen. He gave the bedroom a glance, then dashed through the front room. The front window was wide open. He put his paws on the splintered sill and poked his head out, drippy tongue lolling to one side.

"Down!" gasped Ida. "You'll fall."

Wags dropped to the floor and blinked at her. Ida blinked back. *He obeyed!* Was it just an accident, or had Slick trained him?

"Sit!" said Ida, testing to see.

Wags sat.

"Shake hands."

He lifted his paw.

"Roll over!"

Wags rolled over.

Ida clapped and hugged him. "If it wasn't for the circus, I'd keep you and let Slick have my gunnysack and bottle money. How do you reckon Mr. Trainer'd like those apples?"

Wags licked her face.

Ida giggled and wiped off his kisses and stroked his velvety ears. "Do you want to play circus? I'll make you some tusks, and you can be an elephant."

Ida made the tusks of paper and tied them on with string. Wags chewed up both, putting an end to his elephant career. But he made a good lion. A lyin'-down lion. He had a frightful set of teeth. Ida put her fingers in his mouth when he yawned, and pretended they were her head. The imaginary audience went wild with cheers and claps and whistles.

"Thank you! Thank you! Don't go away, ladies and gentlemen. After intermission the Flying Wards will perform!" she announced through a rolled newspaper.

Ida threw kisses back over her shoulder as she dashed to the bedroom for her good black sateen bloomers. She pulled them on over her old gray ones and tucked her dress inside. The fullness made the black bloomers blouse out like the short spangly romper Jennie Ward wore in the poster on the kitchen wall.

"Ladies and gentlemen, boys and girls, the act you've been waiting for!" she called through her rolled paper. "The famous, the fabulous, the fantastic Flying Wards on the high trapeze!"

Ida jumped off a chair and did handsprings across the floor. Slick had taught her well. She moved so fast, it was almost like flying. The rolled newspaper became a fly bar. She stood on her head on top of it and spread her legs as if her feet were gripping ropes.

Wags struggled up from his dozing to lick her face. Ida collapsed and curled into a ball to avoid his sloppy tongue and wet nose.

"Wags. Quit!" She giggled and dragged her hand across her wet face, then bounded to her feet and took a bow. "That's all for this afternoon, folks! Come back for tonight's show when Wags, the wire-walking dog, will astound and amaze you.

"Oops, sorry, Wags. I forgot. You're scared of heights. Let's have an egg, then you can be a lion again and I'll be the trainer."

Ida straightened her skirt out over her bloomers and went to the kitchen and shared two hard-boiled eggs with Wags.

When they had finished their snack, Ida read an old article from the circus wall: "'Miss Jennie Ward, high trapeze artist with Ringling Brothers' Show, was working without a net during yesterday's performance when she fell forty feet, landing across the wooden ring curb.'

"That's some fall, Wags." Ida turned from the yellowed paper to the dog. "General says you've got to relax and try to let your shoulders take the worst of it. That's what Jennie did. Listen to this," she said, and made room on the chair for Wags. "'Jennie landed on her back and . . .'"

Ida swung around in her chair as Mom came in. Her apron was full of vegetables from their war garden. "Why is that dog in my house?"

"We're pretending he's a lion," hedged Ida.

Mom thumped a head of cabbage down on the table. "No strays, Ida Lou. You know the rules."

"He's Slick's dog. I'm only keeping him until tonight as co-ladder-something-or-other." Ida explained about Slick letting her in on his moneymaking scheme. "Slick's tricky sometimes. But as long as I have Wags, he can't cheat me."

"Maybe you should find a more trustworthy friend," said Mom.

"I've got those kind of friends. But Slick's the only one who knows tumbling."

Mom dumped potatoes into the sink and dusted her hands with a gesture that sent Wags scampering under the table. "Put him out on the fire escape."

"I can't," said Ida. "He's scared of heights."

"Ida!"

"He is, Mom. Really."

"Oh, for pity sake! Leave him, then. But he goes home after supper, no excuses. And no puddles, either. Do you understand me?"

"He wouldn't do that. He's very well behaved. He does tricks, too," said Ida, and named them one by one as she helped Mom prepare vegetables from their war garden.

Mom took Ida's hand as they sat down together at the supper table. She thanked God for food and asked his watch-care over the soldier boys, and her family, too. All except Dad. Mom rarely mentioned him, and never in a praying voice.

There was corn bread to go with the homegrown vegetables. It tasted a lot better to Ida than the coarse-grained

Victory bread they'd been eating so much of since the war began. Midway through lunch, Ida remembered Mr. Trainer complaining over her gouging the wall with the ash bucket and going for the broom, wanting her to sweep up the piddling little anthill of chipped plaster. Mom didn't mention it. Mr. Trainer must not have told her. Yet.

"Are you going to the community sing?" Ida asked, between swallows.

"Not tonight. Lizzy and I want to work on the quilt."

The Liberty Auction was less than a month away. The quilt wasn't finished. But it was looking prettier all the time. It should bring a nice sum for the Red Cross. Ida liked to think she was helping the soldiers in some small way.

"If it wasn't for returning Wags and getting my money from Slick, I'd stay home and quilt," said Ida.

After supper, Ida helped with the dishes, then washed up and put on a clean dress. She was in her room, playing with Wags, when Vic came home. Mom came into the bedroom for her sewing basket. "Vic's changing his clothes," she said, sitting down on the bed. "He's going to eat, then he'll be ready to go."

Mom braided Ida's hair for her and coiled the twin braids, one over each ear. She tied them with faded ribbons, then picked up her sewing basket and left for Aunt Lizzy's.

Vic was ready to go. Wags whined and wouldn't go down the steps. Ida picked him up and started down the fire escape. "Help me, Vic!" she asked when Wags grew heavy.

"I didn't bring him up here," said Vic, a flight ahead of her.

"V-i-i-i-c! Please?"

"Put him down, Ida. He won't fall."

"He might."

"He won't," said Vic, continuing down the stairs without looking back.

Ida sat down on the third landing to rest her arms and catch her breath, then picked Wags up again and carried him all the way to the bottom. By the time she got there, Vic was long gone. She shook the numbness out of her arms.

"Come on, Wags. Let's hurry."

They had just reached the edge of the school grounds when an open touring car stopped in the street that ran in front of the school. Girls in frilly yellow dresses flocked out of it like bees coming out of a hive. They were loud like bees, too. They swarmed toward the sidewalk, waving their arms, squealing.

Wags's ears pricked. Ida gave a start as he bounded toward them, baying like a dog on a fresh rabbit trail.

"Stop, Wags!" she cried. "Come back!"

But Wags didn't stop. He jumped all over the golden-haired girls. There was a boy with them. A man and a woman, too.

"Wherever did you find him?" called the woman over the glad shouts of her children.

"Find him?" echoed Ida, confused.

"We've been looking all day!"

All at once, the truth struck Ida. *Slick!* He was as crooked as Wags's tail! He had tricked her! He'd taken her bottles and sack and tricked her! It wasn't his dog at all!

Chapter Nine

Lots of folks were filing into the school building. But the singing hadn't started yet. Slick would be on the playground. *If he showed up at all. The low-down sneak!*

Ida pounded around to the back of the building. The swing set sprawled over the scorched grass like a giant, long-legged spider. Children swarmed on the attached swings and trapezes and ladders. And there was Slick, hanging by his knees from the overhead crossbar.

"Skin the Cat, Slick!" called a young admirer from the ground.

"Yeah, Skin the Cat! Skin the Cat!" the others took up the chant.

Skin his hide! Ida clenched her fists and shouldered her way through. She stopped directly under Slick. "Slick Baumgart, come here, you big, fat fibber!"

"Hey, Ida!" Slick waved at her from his upside-down position. "Let's see you do this."

"Wags isn't your dog!"

"Oh, that," said Slick smoothly. "I never said he was. You just jumped to that conclusion."

"Because you made me! You're worse than a sometimes-friend! You're no friend at all!"

"I taught you handsprings, didn't I?" said Slick, red-faced from dangling by one knee. "And for free, too."

"Free? What about all the eggs you ate?"

"They want legal tender at the Y."

Ida didn't know what "legal tender" meant. Slick knew a lot of words she didn't know. It was part of his trickery. "How much money did you get for my bottle and sack?"

"Four cents."

"Hand it over."

"Just a second. I'm coming." Slick swung into an upright position. He moved hand over hand toward a leg of the gym set and slid to the ground beside her. "Can you meet me at the dump tomorrow?"

"You said meet you here, and I'm here. I want my money!"

"I came up a little short paying for my tumbling lessons," he admitted.

"Doggone it, Slick! You've done it now!" Ida pivoted and tramped toward the school.

"Where are you going?"

"To get Vic."

"Aw, Ida! Since when did you turn into a tattletale?"

"Since you took my money!" said Ida.

"I didn't think you'd care since the lessons help you, too," said Slick, hurrying to catch up.

"But I do care!" Ida turned so abruptly, Slick's nose bumped her forehead. "We made a deal!"

"Tumbling lessons are a good investment," he said. "We'll share the dividends."

"Divi-what? I don't want divi-anything. I want a circus ticket!"

"I'll go to the dump tomorrow and find some stuff, and pay you back. How's that?"

"You think I'm falling for that?"

"Honest," said Slick.

Honest. That was *one* word Slick Baumgart *didn't* know! Not the true meaning, anyway. Ida opened her mouth to tell him so when someone tapped her on the shoulder. She swung around to see the boy she had met earlier. The boy with all the sisters. Wags's boy.

"Here," he said. "Father said to give you this for finding our dog Swisher."

He dropped a silver dollar in her hand. It gleamed in the sunlight. The surprise of it sucked the breath out of Ida's lungs. It was all she could do to thank him.

"Where did you find him?" he asked.

"At the dump."

"We found him together," said Slick, right quick.

"Thanks," said the boy. He returned Slick's crocodile smile.

Ha! thought Ida at Slick's crestfallen look. She thrust the dollar into her pocket and kept her hand on it. The music started inside. The boy waved and ran toward the building where his family was waiting. The rest of the children on the playground bounded in that direction, too. Ida waited. Slick did, too. He hooked his hands in his suspenders and rocked back on his heels.

"Just think," he said. "If if wasn't for me, you wouldn't have that dollar."

"No. I'd have a dollar and four cents!" countered Ida.

"Some friend *you* are," he said, and let his shoulders slump as he turned away.

It was supposed to make her feel selfish. It might have, too, except Slick sneaked a glance to see if it was working. Ida poked her tongue out at him.

The dollar was warm and weighty in her hand. She kissed Lady Liberty, flipped the coin, and kissed the eagle, too. Hallelujah, hurrah! She was rich! Nothing could keep her from seeing the circus now!

Chapter Ten

Ida was too excited to sit in a stuffy gymnasium full of hot people. She stayed on the playground, climbed on the trapeze, and sailed through the clover-sweet air.

"Howdy-doody, Ida Lou."

"General!" Ida flipped to the ground and ran to meet him. "Are you going inside?"

"No, magirl. I'm just walking off dinner. They're in fine voice, aren't they?" General sat down in a swing as music poured out the auditorium windows. "Them and us music, fit to whip the kaiser."

He sighed. *Because he couldn't sing?* Ida looked at his scarred throat and settled into the swing next to his. "I could sing for you if you want."

"Now there's a thought." General smiled. "Sing for the doughboys. Sing loud enough for both of us."

Ida sang. She knew all the words from months of listening to Vic. Her singing sounded so good, she put her fingers in her ears and blocked out all the other voices.

General whistled and tapped his feet. Crickets chorused from hidden places, and fireflies lifted from the grass. Then the sun melted away, and the music stopped.

Vic filed out into the dusky schoolyard with some friends. He waved to General and called to Ida, "We're going over to read the war bulletins. Tell Mom I'll be home after a while."

Vic knew boys fighting in France. He watched for their names on the public bulletins posted at the newspaper office. Ida turned homeward at General's side.

They arrived to find Aunt Lizzy on her knees in a tight squeeze between General's trunk and the quilting frame. Pointing under the frame, she said, "Help me, Ida. My thread has rolled out of reach."

Ida crawled under and retrieved the spool.

"Thank you, dear." Aunt Lizzy drew Ida into her arms and smothered her in scents of lilac water and face powder.

"Where's Mom?" asked Ida, hugging her back. "Did she go home already?"

"No. She's upstairs," said Aunt Lizzy. "Mr. Trainer is having trouble hiring paperhangers, what with so many tradesmen gone to war. Your mother's sizing up the job, seeing if she's equal to it."

At the sound of voices, Ida swung around and looked just as the door opened a crack. Hearing Mr. Trainer's low rumble, she got hot and itchy over the ash bucket incident. But Mom came in alone.

Ida passed along Vic's message. She showed off her dollar and repeated the whole story of Slick's trickery, a lost dog, and a grateful family's generosity.

"My stars! A dollar! That *was* generous." Mom sat down at the quilting frame and handed Ida a needle. "Thread it, would you? My eyes are tired."

Her eyes didn't look tired. They looked sparkly. So

did the rest of her face. A wrinkle surfaced on the edge of Ida's contentment. But General chased it away, saying, "Thread one for me, too, Ida Loody."

Ida perched on General's trunk. There were clothes on it. Aunt Lizzy pitched them to one side, warning, "Careful! Those are full of dust! General can't seem to remember to wear dungarees for heavy jobs."

"Dungarees?" echoed General. "Must have packed them away with my circus togs. Maybe Bertha knows what's become of them," he added with a twinkle in his eye.

"Bertha?" echoed Ida.

"The bull," said General. "I loaned her my trunk. You didn't think she grew it, surely?"

In the circus, even female elephants were "bulls." Ida handed him his needle and asked, without daring to look at Mom, "Can I see inside?"

"My advice is never look a bull in the snout, magirl."

"Not that trunk. This trunk!" said Ida, tapping the lid.

"Ida, quit aggravating General," said Mom.

"Ida? Aggravate? Never!" General rallied to her defense. "She's on a treasure hunt, is all." But he didn't offer to let Ida see inside.

"General?" asked Ida. "Do you have any pictures of your circus days?"

"I did at one time, magirl. But I lost them in the fire."

"What fire?"

"The fire of reform Lizzy lit under me when she got down on her knees and proposed," said General.

"Malarkey!" sputtered Aunt Lizzy.

Their playfulness soothed Ida's disappointment in being denied yet again a glimpse into the tangibles of General's circus past.

Needles plucked and threads whispered. Voices rose and fell. Spurts of laughter, too, at General's patter of circus yarns. His "jackpot," he called it.

Ida yawned in cozy contentment and wished that General would take her to the circus where he used to work, and say, "This is magirl, Ida Lou, and she wants to fly."

Then, they'd travel around the country together, her and General and Mom and Aunt Lizzy. And Vic, too, if he wanted to go instead of making candy for Mr. Beich.

Life would be just about perfect, then.

Chapter Eleven

Ida ate an early breakfast with Vic the next morning. She told him about Wags not really belonging to Slick, and how the boy and his golden sisters leaped out of the automobile and ran to claim their pet.

"Then, he went and spent my bottle and sack money on his tumbling lessons," she said, jabbing the eye of her soft-cooked egg. "But he's *done* tricking me! See here?" Ida slapped the silver dollar down on the table and finished her story.

"Slick didn't want a cut?"

"'Course he did. But I didn't give it to him."

"So you beat him at his own game, did you? Pretty shrewd."

Pleased, Ida said, "Mom won't let me go to the circus alone. How about going with me, Vic? I'll buy your ticket."

"You?" A surprised grin lit Vic's face. "You're all right, Ida."

"All righta-Ida!" Ida laughed and leaped out of her chair and followed him to the door. "Let's see the sideshow, too."

"If your money stretches that far," said Vic. He grabbed his dinner bucket and cap.

"And drink pink lemonade!" Ida said, trailing him out on the landing.

Vic waved on his way down. "See you later, circus girl."

"Bye, candy boy," called Ida, leaning over the railing.

Ida sang as she washed dishes and dumped the pan of water that had collected under the icebox. She was putting on her shoes when Mom came upstairs and told her to weed the war garden.

"But I was just going down to help General."

"General has already gone," said Mom. "He left a little while ago."

"Without me?"

"There's a lot of plaster to haul. You'll have plenty of chances to help," said Mom. She tidied her hair and changed her apron and started back through the front room. "I'll be hanging wallpaper one floor down if you need me."

Ida wrinkled her nose. "Work, work. Mr. Trainer is good about making work for other people."

"Just weed the garden, Ida Lou. The green beans are ready. Pick enough for General and Lizzy, too," added Mom on her way out.

The war garden they shared with General and Aunt Lizzy was behind the building on a vacant lot. It was planted over the buried rubble of a building that had burned a long time ago. Hoeing always turned up bits of glass, brick, stone, broken china, and other relics. Ida pretended she was on a treasure hunt. Time slipped by as she examined each "find."

It was hot when Ida finished her job. She trekked upstairs, washed and sliced a raw potato, and crossed to the pantry for the salt shaker. Vic's clothes hung from a rod that passed through the middle of the pantry. Ida shoved them to one side when Slick hollered to her from the landing.

"Slick? What're *you* doing here?"

"Brought you something." Slick let himself in and dropped four cents on the kitchen table.

Ida stepped out of the pantry, salt shaker in hand. She checked the pennies to make sure they weren't metal buttons or something else tricky.

"So *now* what do you say?"

"Thanks," said Ida, satisfied they were real.

"Besides that."

"That you're not so low-down after all?"

"I'm talking about the dollar for finding the lost dog."

"It was me who took care of Wags yesterday, remember?" Ida pushed a potato slice into her mouth and punctuated his silence with crunching noises. "Want a slice?"

"That's decent of you," he said, and held out his hand.

"Of *potato*," she said, salting another piece.

"Oh." Slick ate the potato slice, then poked his nosy head into the pantry. "Hey! I've got an idea."

"Those are Vic's, you'd better leave them alone," warned Ida as Slick moved the clothes from the rod to a kitchen chair.

"I'll put them back. Watch this." Slick chinned himself on the pantry rod. "Just as I thought. Plenty solid. You want a turn? Go on, try it!"

Ida wrapped her hands around the bar and pulled herself off the floor. "Not bad," she admitted, and counted off chin-ups, " . . . eight, nine, ten."

"Aunt Pliney can do more than that. You'd better grow some muscle."

"I've got plenty of muscle! When I join out, I'm going straight to the low-grass. That's—"

"Circus parlance for city," said Slick. "I know."

Parlance? Ida sniffed and said, "Watch me Skin the Cat."

"I'll not only watch, I'll help you improve your style, for a stipend. Know what *that* is?"

"Doesn't everybody?" bluffed Ida.

Slick flashed a grin and jumped into action. "First, clear out the canned goods; I'll get the dishes. Give you more room to work."

"Okay," said Ida. "But we have to put everything back before Mom comes home."

They emptied the pantry in record time. The shelf boards weren't nailed down. They lifted out easily. The pantry looked a lot bigger without them. The rod, to Ida's delight, was just the right height.

"I'll be right back." Ida ducked into her bedroom and closed the door to re-create yesterday's costume.

When she returned, Slick darted two skippity glances, like maybe he'd seen wrong the first time.

"It's my circus costume," said Ida quickly.

"I figured that out," said Slick. He crossed to the sink, snitched a red radish, and said, "Are you ready?"

"Almost." Ida sprinkled ARGO starch on her hands. It made them look chalky, like aerialists' hands should. She bent her elbows and stacked her arms, one over the other, in front of her chest, standing just like Jennie Ward did on her circus wall.

"What're you waiting for?" asked Slick.

"You're the ringmaster. Announce my act."

"Ringmaster? Huh-uh. I'm just here for the stipend, remember?"

"Never mind, I'll do it myself. Introducing the newest member of the Flying Wards, Florida Louisa Ward!" Ida gripped the rod, swung her legs up between her arms, and let go with her hands. "Ta-da! You can clap now."

"What for?" asked Slick.

"Because you're the audience."

"No, I'm not. I'm not playing, I'm working."

Ida scowled from her upside-down position. "Wags was more fun than you."

"So? He wasn't on the clock. Let's see you do a Bird's Nest."

Ida arched her back and gripped her ankles over the top of the bar, with her stomach facing the floor. "What clock?"

"Arch your back!"

"I'm trying, but my arms are getting tired. What clock?"

"The time clock. That's parlance for pay," added Slick.

"Pay? Huh-uh! I never said anything about paying you!"

"Sure, you did. I said I'd help for a stipend, and you agreed."

"I did not! Help me, I'm—" Ida's hands slipped. She belly flopped to the floor and couldn't get her breath.

Slick hunkered down, forearms on his knees. "See what happens when your mind wanders? Lesson number one: Pay attention to what you're doing."

Ida raised her stinging chin from the floor in windless outrage.

"That's all for today," said Slick. "I'll take my stipend and be on my way."

"Hey!" cried Ida, finding her breath as he scooped the four cents from the table. "That's not fair!"

"Sure it is. I earned it." Slick closed her into the pantry before she could stumble out.

Ida pounded on the rickety door. "Let me out! It's hot in here! I can't breathe."

"Admit I earned it, and I'll let you out."

Ida clamped her jaw tight, switched tactics, and slumped to the floor. She lay so still, she heard Slick's overalls rustle as he squatted down on the other side of the door.

"Ida?" He reached under the wide crack in the door and touched her fingertips. "You'd better speak up, or I'm going to stick your fingers in this mousetrap."

Ida knew better. She didn't twitch, not even when he pinched one fingertip between his fingernails.

"Maybe I'll just barricade you in and go home," he

said, and pinched her again. "Or did you want to admit I earned my pay?"

She'd smother first! Footsteps came on the heels of that thought. Frightened he really had locked her in, Ida raised up on one elbow. "Slick? Don't you dare! Slick?" She pushed the pantry door. It swung open without resistance.

"Ida Lou? What was that awful racket?"

Mom! Ida leaped to her feet just as her mother strode through the kitchen door.

Slick was gone.

Chapter Twelve

Mom stopped short. She looked as if she had the wind knocked out of her, too.

Ida surveyed the messy kitchen and said in a rush, "I'm going to put it all back."

"What *are* you doing?"

"Playing circus," said Ida.

"For goodness' sake! It sounded like you were coming through the floor! Pull your skirt out of your bloomers."

Ida couldn't wiggle out of the black bloomers fast enough.

"What is this you've tracked in?"

"Starch. I put it on my hands. I'm pretending it's rosin like circus girls use."

Ida smoothed her skirts as Mom followed the trail of starch into the pantry and ran her hand along the rod. She swung around, her face almost as white as her starchy palms. "I-da-Lou! Have you been playing on this pipe?"

"Pipe? I thought it was a closet rod," said Ida, her voice shrinking.

"It's a water pipe!"

"But Vic hangs his clothes there."

Mom clapped her hand to her forehead in dismay. "A few shirts and a swinging girl are not the same thing at all! You had better hope it doesn't spring a leak! How would I explain it to Herman?"

"Herman?"

Mom went right on scolding. She didn't even notice she'd called Mr. Trainer by his first name. Ida picked up a shelf board and returned it to the pantry. Her heart jumped as something wet hit her foot. But it was her eyes, not the pipe, that were leaking. A second tear slid down her cheek, dropped off her chin, and landed on her bare foot.

"Good gracious! Who would ever guess you'd have to be told not to swing on a pipe? Where do you get these ideas, anyway?"

"Slick said it was sturdy. He never once said it was a water pipe."

"Slick?" Mom's tone struck a new note. "He was here? And you, in your bloomers!"

"It's a costume." Ida pointed to Jennie's shining image on the circus wall.

"Your skirt in your underwear is not a costume, Ida Lou! And in front of Slick! Why was he here, anyway?"

"I didn't invite him, he just came," said Ida, rubbing her itchy eyes.

"Next time, tell Slick you can't have friends in unless I'm here. You're old enough to realize keeping a good name doesn't happen by accident. You don't want folks whispering about you, do you?"

Mom's tone made it clear that whisperings wouldn't be compliments. Ida's cheeks burned. Another tear splatted on her powdery toes. "He was just helping me. He wants to be in the circus, too."

"Everyone dreams, Ida Lou. But the point is—"

"Even you?" asked Ida.

"Of course."

"Is Mr. Trainer in your dreams?" Ida put words to a naggy feeling that curled like a leaf from the ground when she'd heard Mr. Trainer and Mom laughing together outside General's apartment the night before.

Mom's cheeks turned pink. "We aren't talking about me, we're talking about you. Now clean up this mess, and when I come upstairs again, I expect to find the green beans snapped and everything in order."

Without Slick to help, it took Ida a lot longer to put things back than it had to drag them out. It was late in the afternoon when she finally got around to the green beans. The heat upstairs drove her outdoors into the shade on the fire escape.

General Useful was in the alley below, unhitching Josephine from the wagon. "Howdy do, magirl," he said as she settled on the bottom step.

"Hi."

General knocked the dust off his trousers and sat down beside her. "Are you needing some help with those beans? Put 'em down here between us, then, and no sticking 'em in your ears." At her failed smile, he reached for a handful of beans, asking, "Is there trouble under the big top?"

"Slick," grumbled Ida.

"I saw him out at the dump this morning. He said he was coming to pay off his debts."

"He paid me, all right. Then took it back again," huffed Ida.

"He did, did he? On what grounds?"

Ida told him about Slick tricking her with his fancy word for "pay," and how he'd closed her in the pantry, then run off and left her to face Mom's scolding and the mess all alone.

General clucked his tongue in sympathy. "That boy has a gift for grift that bears watching."

"Yep. What's grift?" said Ida, all in the same breath.

"Grift, madear, is shady dealings."

"Like cheating with tricky words?"

"That's one way," said General.

"There's others?"

"As many as there are folks to try them. Tigers aren't the only cats with claws."

General's understanding manner soothed Ida's scratched feelings. She pretended that under those scars he was Dad, aged by the hard time he'd had since running off. And that he had come back, heart sorry for running off, and that he was only pretending to be married to Aunt Lizzy so he could be close to Mom and Vic and her, and that he went by General Useful because he was afraid to say who he *really* was, on account of Mom's good-riddance voice.

"A billion and six, a billion seven. I'm gaining on you, magirl," said General, making a race of their work, and a contest of who was going to get the last bean.

Ida snatched the last one from the dishpan, snapped it quick, and threw her arms in the air. "I win!"

"Oh, do you now?" Eyes twinkling, General reached behind her ear. "What's this, magirl?"

Ida giggled and grabbed the bean from his hand and crammed it in her mouth. "Where? What bean?"

General sighed. "I concede. You're Queen Green Bean!"

"Ta-da!" Ida giggled and took her bow and wiped green bean juice off her chin.

General winked and brushed the clingy green bean tips and tails from his trousers, then crossed to the basement window and called to Aunt Lizzy, saying he was taking Josephine to the livery.

Ida didn't catch Aunt Lizzy's reply. She was dreaming again, forming up a happy ending where General revealed his true identity, and Aunt Lizzy said she knew all along, and Mom forgave them both.

"Ida Lou?" called Aunt Lizzy from the basement window.

"Right here, Aunt Lizzy." Ida skipped to the window, then turned and waved to General as he rode the singletree down the alley, the long lines looped in his hands.

"Bring the green beans in, darling," said Aunt Lizzy. "Your mama isn't going to feel like cooking after wallpapering all day."

"There's potatoes and onions upstairs," said Ida. "And some radishes, too."

"Run and get them," said Aunt Lizzy. "And tell Anna supper will be ready about six."

Chapter Thirteen

Vic was washing up at the sink, splashing water on Ida, when General beat a tin plate at the bottom of the stairs. "Flag's up!" he hollered. "Come and get it!"

"That's circus talk for—"

"Supper," said Vic. "If you'd pay half as much attention in school as you do to General's circus jackpot, you might amount to something someday."

"I pay attention!"

"Then how come Slick hoodwinks you with big words? Explain that," he said, and left with a dish of deviled eggs.

Feelings smarting, Ida tossed the salad Mom had made of fresh garden lettuce and diced vegetables. She was on her way downstairs when Mom paused on the stairs and waved to Mr. Trainer in the alley below. His motorcar had been parked out back all day.

"He helped with the wallpapering," said Mom when Ida asked. "Watch the salad, you're tilting the bowl," she added, and took it from her.

Aunt Lizzy's kitchen was hot, so they ate on the shady fire escape steps. After supper, Vic and General brought the quilting frame outside, where it was cooler. Crickets chirped. Passing streetcars clanged. The courthouse clock rang the hour as the day's troubles washed clean in a potluck of laughter and lazy conversation.

"Don't forget to wake me up in the morning," Ida called to Vic as he ambled off to look up some friends.

"Are you going to watch the circus unload?" asked General, joining Mom and Aunt Lizzy at the quilting frame.

"Yep!" said Ida. "You'll be there, won't you?"

"But of course!"

"Just don't forget to come home," said Aunt Lizzy.

"What do you take me for, my pet?" asked General, doing his best to look injured.

"I knew a young man once who ran off with the circus." Aunt Lizzy looked over the tops of her sewing glasses. "His family had a hard time harvesting without him that year."

"Hey, Mom?" said Ida. "Dad farmed for a while, didn't he?"

"If you count wild oats," said Mom.

"Anna!" murmured Aunt Lizzy. She fanned her shiny face and urged Ida to help with the quilting.

Ida traced a star, liking the tufted feel of it beneath her fingertips. She threaded a needle and settled into daydreams, quilting with an even stitch as Mom and Lizzy traded meatless, wheatless recipes. General plucked along in silence, then tied off his thread and reached for the spool.

Ida looked up to see him making a long-armed, squinting, one-eyed aim at the needle. "When did they start making such small-eyed needles?"

Ida giggled and offered, "Want me to?"

"No, no, I'll not be bested by a bit of steel," said General. "Did I ever tell you about the needle-snouted creature who traveled with the menagerie back in my roustabout days? Oh, he was a fearful-looking thing. It caused quite a stir the day he escaped and tumbled fences and browsed backyards of a dirty little mining town."

"Did you catch him?" asked Ida, using up the last stitch on her thread.

"We did. After he had cleared every clothesline in town," claimed General. "There were enough red-flannels pegged to that snout of his to keep the joeys in cold-weather togs for three seasons. Now that's a needle. No skimpy bit of eyeless steel!"

Joeys were clowns. Ida laughed so hard, she didn't realize the thread General was threading was still attached to the spool. She grabbed the spool, pulling the thread right out of his needle.

"By golly, magirl, I won't take much more of that!" he exclaimed with a comic start.

Mom and Aunt Lizzy tittered and wiped their eyes and laughed some more. Ida swallowed the last of her giggles and looked up to see some friends tramping up the alley, toting stick guns and arguing over whose turn it was to be the enemy.

"Can you play, Ida Lou?" called one of the boys.

"Go on, magirl! Whip the kaiser," urged General.

Ida jumped up and tied Mom's apron to her head and joined their war game as a Red Cross nurse. The Yanks made the garden no-man's-land. The weeds Ida had uprooted that morning became enemy soldiers.

Ida leaped trenches and hauled wounded to her field hospital under the fire escape. She bandaged heads and saved bleeding limbs with rags and stick tourniquets.

Then the sun set and the Yanks marched away, and Ida peeled the apron off her sweaty brow.

Mom helped General and Aunt Lizzy carry the quilting frame inside. Ida was waiting on the step when headlamps turned up the alley and trapped her in their glare. The motorcar stopped a few yards away.

"Is your mother here?" called Mr. Trainer from behind the wheel.

"She's inside with Aunt Lizzy and General," said Ida, shielding her eyes. He climbed out. She remembered Mom waving to him from the landing earlier, and was tempted to wait and see what he wanted. But then she thought of yesterday's gouged plaster and changed her mind.

"Herman, Herman, rhymes with German," she hummed all the way up the stairs. But, one foot into the kitchen, trouble, *real* trouble, washed the chant from her mind. Water! Everywhere!

Ida slid across the wet floor and opened the pantry door. Water oozed from the pipe. It trailed over Vic's soppy clothes. It ran under the door and gathered in puddles trapped in valleys and sinkholes in the uneven floor.

Ida puddle-jumped to the landing to bellow for help. But Mr. Trainer's motorcar stopped her cold. She raced back to the pantry, tied a rag to the pipe, fit the broomstick in the knot, and gave it a twist. It stopped bleeding limbs in Yanks and nurse games. Would it stop a leaky pipe?

"Please, please!" she prayed, and held her breath, watching. But the dampness spread over the rag, then plip, plip, plip. Oh boy, was she in trouble!

Ida slapped through the water back to the fire escape.

Mom was strolling toward the war garden at Mr. Trainer's side. Out of ideas, Ida galloped down the stairs, bellowing for help.

Mom swung around. "What is it, Ida?"

"The pipe! In the pantry. Come quick!"

Mom came at a run. Mr. Trainer, too. Ida ran down. They ran up.

"How bad is it?" asked Mom, huffing for air as they met on the middle landing.

"Bad."

"Oh, my stars! I was afraid of this!"

"It's leaked before?" asked Mr. Trainer.

"Ida swung on it."

"She *what?*"

"She swung on it."

"Great guns! What'd you do that for?"

"I thought it was—"

"The shutoff valve?" he cut her short, shooting the question to Mom.

"In the basement, I suppose. General would know," Mom called after him as he raced back down the steps.

Ida sank to the steps and burst into tears.

"Oh, no, you don't! You march up here right now!" Mom clutched her skirts and kept climbing.

Ida heard the water from the open door.

"Don't just stand there! Grab rags and start sopping it up before it runs through the floor," ordered Mom on her rush to the pantry.

Only then did Ida remember the freshly papered walls and ceiling, just one floor below.

Chapter Fourteen

Mr. Trainer stopped in the open door moments later. It was the first he'd seen of their apartment. Ida caught her breath as his train-beam gaze swept the newspapered walls, the crumbling ceiling, the saggy, soggy floor.

"Did you find General?" asked Mom. She was on her knees, mopping.

Mr. Trainer strode past her without a word. He made a turn through the front room, then retraced his steps to the kitchen and met Mom's wary expression. "Why didn't you say something?" he asked.

"About what?"

"This dismal eyesore!"

"I'm grateful for the shelter," said Mom.

"Grateful?" he exclaimed, voice rising. "The ceiling's falling in, the walls are crumbling, the floor is weak. Great guns, Anna! This place is in shambles!"

"The hall mop is downstairs, if you want to help."

"A mop isn't going to fix it! " he cut in. "Summers said it was utilitarian. He didn't say it was falling in."

"He was trying to help."

"Some help."

"I pressed him for it," said Mom. "I didn't take it sight unseen."

"Then he took advantage of your desperation."

Mom flinched, her work-worn hands stalling on the rag she was using to sop up water.

"I'm sorry," he said quickly. "That was uncalled for. It's just that I had no idea it was in this condition. Surely you must understand that you can't go on living here with plaster hanging in ribbons. You'll wake up some morning with the ceiling around your ears!"

"I'm sorry about the pipe," Mom talked right over him, the way she used to do when Dad had something to say that she didn't want to hear. "I'll pay for the damages."

"Would you listen to me?" demanded Mr. Trainer. "I don't see how I can let you go on living here the way it is. Not in good conscience, anyway."

"Good conscience?" countered Mom. She came to her feet, a warning glint in her eye. "What in good conscience *can* you do? Put us out in the street?"

"There are other options, Anna."

Mom turned her back on him and said to Ida, "Go get General."

"He isn't here, I sent him for a plumber," said Mr. Trainer. "I was about to say that if you're set on staying, which it seems you are, I'll bring in carpenters and do the job right."

"I don't want to be in your debt."

"They've been in the building for a month, ripping and pounding. Has that put you in my debt?"

"It isn't the same thing, and you know it."

"How is it different? Go on. Speak plainly," he urged.

"I can't take charity," said Mom, her voice as stiff as her spine.

"Is it charity you're rejecting? Or the face behind it?"

Mom's color returned in one bright wave. "You don't know what you're saying!"

"I know well enough. The problem is, I'm saying it badly."

"I'm the cleaning lady!"

"Yes?" he prompted.

"You own the building!"

"Yes."

Mom darted Ida a wild-eyed glance, then set her jaw and said, "I need a mop."

"I'll get it," said Ida, anxious to escape the tension.

"Take your time," said Mr. Trainer.

Ida knew, then, that they weren't done fighting. Would he fix the place up? Or kick them out? If he did, it would be her fault for swinging on the pipe. What would they do? Where would they live?

Ida's feet squeaked all the way to the door.

When Ida returned, there were wet towels and rags on the landing and in the sink and no sign of Mom. Mr. Trainer had his back to her, his sleeves rolled up. His wrench on the pipe made grinding noises that reminded her of fingernails on blackboards. Goose bumps tickled her spine and prickled down her arms. She set the mop and bucket down and tiptoed into the front room.

Mom wasn't there. The bedroom was empty, too. On impulse, Ida dropped to her knees and reached under her bed for her rusty trapeze. She gripped it in sweaty hands. Her palm left a rusty smear on the sheet as she came to her feet.

"If you're looking for your mother, she's downstairs," said Mr. Trainer from the kitchen.

Ida didn't answer.

"Come out here a minute."

Ida took the bar with her. She stopped three feet from the open pantry door.

"She's worried about water damage below," said Mr. Trainer, though Ida hadn't asked.

Ida said what she'd tried to say before: "I thought it was a closet rod."

"Anna explained. Closet rods aren't for swinging, either."

The wrench slipped from Mr. Trainer's hand. Ida jumped as it hit the floor. He picked it up and stepped out of the pantry. His face was sweaty; his hair was damp, too. He wiped his face on his sleeve and pushed a chair her way. "Sit down."

Ida sat.

He pulled up another chair and sat down, facing her. "There are going to be some changes."

Ida stopped swinging her feet.

Mr. Trainer rocked forward, resting his forearms on his knees, his eyes level with hers. "I've asked your mother to marry me."

Ida's hands tightened on the trapeze. "She's married," she said.

"Deserted, is what she is, Ida." Into her silence, he

added, "There are courts of law for that. A divorce will be granted, and she'll be free to marry again."

Divorce. The word hit the air like the sound of ice cracking underfoot. *Divorce. Divorce. Divorce*, it echoed.

"In the meantime, Vic's going back to school," Mr. Trainer was saying. "He doesn't know it yet, but he is."

His mention of Vic reminded Ida of Vic's sorrow the day he had quit school. But that was a long time ago. He liked working for Mr. Beich. He was happy now. They didn't need Mr. Trainer. He would only be in the way.

"What about you?"

Ida lifted her face. She hadn't been listening. He was waiting. She had no idea for what. "Would you like to go to the circus tomorrow?" he asked.

"I *am* going. With Vic."

"If you can wait until evening, we'll go together," he said. "Your mother and me and you and Vic. You can see the menagerie, too. And eat hot dogs for supper and take an elephant ride, if you like."

Ida had seen other kids ride elephants and buy hot dogs and lemonade and circus candy, and still have money left for the kid show. She envied them. And acknowledged Mr. Trainer's cleverness. He was a fixer. A fixer-upper. But some things couldn't be fixed with wrenches and carpenters and money for the kid show. Especially not if it meant cutting out other people. Like Dad.

"I'll go with Vic, the way we planned," she said.

Mr. Trainer slid the wrench to the table. He sat back in his chair. "My father taught me that success hinges on getting along with people. And not just in business. I learned that I could, if I made up my mind to. What about you, Ida? Can you get along with me?"

Ida ducked her head and didn't answer.

"Is there something to lose by trying?" he pressed.

She gripped her bar and waited him out. It was so quiet that she heard General stop Josephine in the alley below. Mr. Trainer came to his feet and left by the fire escape.

"There's a place on the ceiling that will have to be touched up," called Mom as she came in the front way. "But otherwise, the room below seems to have escaped water damage. Thank goodness." She swept a hand through faded hair, poked her head in the pantry and out again. "Where's Herman?"

"General's back. He went to see if he brought a plumber with him."

Mom nodded. Ida studied her closely. Her eyes were red, but dry. Her face was white, but wet. She looked tired, not beaten. Ida wanted to ask about Dad. About divorce. But the words were too raw. The possibilities too scary.

In a moment, Mr. Trainer returned. General was with him. He had a pipe and some fittings and tools, but no plumber. Vic came home and offered his help.

Mom sent Ida to bed. She lay in the airless bedroom, hot and sweaty and tired. Eventually, she slept.

Ida didn't hear Mom come to bed. But she turned and found her curled up beside her. The pipe-banging had stopped. The voices, too. Ida's slumbering thoughts stirred. Under cover of darkness, she whispered, "Mom? Are you marrying Mr. Trainer?"

"He doesn't know what he's asking," said Mom without giving an answer. "How could he? He's never been married, much less had children depending on him."

"What if Dad comes back?"

Mom rolled over, her back to Ida.

"Mom?" whispered Ida.

"Go to sleep, Ida," said Mom. "We'll talk when I'm not so tired."

Chapter Fifteen

"Come on if you're coming," said Vic, shaking Ida's shoulder. "I'll wait downstairs."

Ida was stiff and sore and uneasy. It wasn't until she walked into the kitchen and saw Mr. Trainer's wrench on the table that she remembered why. She dressed quickly, tucked eggs in her pocket, and galloped down the stairs to catch up with Vic.

Buildings loomed like giants, washed in patches of lamplight. Ida walked in their shadows, eating a hard-boiled egg. She peeled one for Vic.

"No thanks," he said when she offered it. "I'm sick of eggs."

"Not me," said Ida. "It's the only nice thing about Mr. Trainer."

"He's not so bad," said Vic, the way he always did.

"You're just saying that 'cause he's sending you back to school."

"Who told you that?" countered Vic.

"He did. He says he's going to marry Mom."

"I know," said Vic. "Mom told me."

"When?"

"Last night, after he left."

"What'd she say?"

"She asked me what I thought, is all, and I told her."

"Not to?"

"No," said Vic. "Why would I? It's her choice, not mine."

"What about Dad?"

"You're beating a dead horse," said Vic.

"Huh?"

"Dad isn't coming back."

"You don't know that for sure," argued Ida.

"I know Mom, and she isn't about to forget."

"Forget what?"

Vic was a long time without answering.

"What?" insisted Ida. "Tell me!"

"Dad wasn't alone when he left."

Confused, Ida said, "He went on a train. Of course he wasn't alone."

"He wasn't *working* on the train, though. He bought a ticket and left with another . . . gal."

It was like a hole opening in the ground. A black hole filled with dark crawly things. Ida rubbed her eyes and made the hole go away. What Vic said couldn't be right. Dad was Dad. He didn't do bad things. There had to be a reason. A misunderstanding.

Or maybe Mom had said it because she was angry for weeks before and after Dad went away. And she *was* angry. Ida remembered raised voices waking her in the night.

"Did Mom tell you that?"

Vic shook his head. "But people talk, you know?"

Ida kicked at a stone. Wanted to kick Vic, too, and make him take back what he'd said. Instead, she said, "I hate trains."

"Then what're we doing, walking to the station at four in the morning?"

Ida's throat hurt when she swallowed. She batted stinging eyes. Once, when she was smaller, she had put her hand in her pocket so Mom wouldn't know she had burned it, playing with the stove. It throbbed so badly, she wouldn't take it out and look at it for fear her fingers had fallen off.

Vic's words about Dad were that way. She crowded them into a dark corner. Closed curtains. Bolted doors. And broke into a trot.

The lights of the station beamed in the distance. The train was in! Lit by flares and torches and railroad lights and lanterns, it stretched into the darkness like a dusty serpent. Ida stopped well short of it. Behind bright curlicues and painted letters, it was still a train. Spooky, to Ida. Yet enticing, too.

Already, a big crowd had gathered to see it unload. Ironclad wheels rolled and creaked. Hard-muscled men heaved and pushed and sweated and shouted, unloading the wagons on twin ramps called runs. Men stepped out of the shadows and hitched teams to the wagons. Teamsters climbed aboard and drove away, headed for the circus grounds.

Vic caught up with Ida. Slick found her, too. He bumped her shoulder in greeting.

Ida pushed him back. "That wasn't a closet rod you swung on!" she said, glad for a reason to yell. "It was a pipe, and it broke."

"Me? You swung on it, too."

"Only because you said it was all right. It wasn't. It made an awful mess!"

"How was I to know?" he asked.

"You acted like you did."

"Did you get in trouble?"

"What do you think?" said Ida.

"Go someplace else, if you're going to fight," ordered Vic, elbowing her. "That's Mr. Beich over there."

Ida sniffed. Her anger with Slick dulled, crowded out by Mr. Trainer and Mom and Dad and things she wasn't looking at. She heard jangling chains and looked for elephants. But it was just an ordinary-looking wagon, coming down the runs.

"I'll bet the cook tent's inside. They have to get it set up first, so their people can eat." Slick rubbed his stomach and asked, "Did you bring any eggs with you?"

Ida gave him the last one.

He took it, thanked her, and swung off down the siding.

"Where you going?"

"I want to see the rest," he called back.

"Go on, if you want to," said Vic, seeming eager to be rid of her.

Slick was in deep shadow by the time Ida caught up with him. He scrambled over the coupling between two cars, then stopped on the other side and motioned to her. "Come on. The sleeper cars are over here."

Ida saw the second section of train on the next siding. She had to touch train things to cross over. She jumped clear, and shook off the feeling of chilled fingers on her spine.

Slick had his hands in his pockets and his head thrown back as he looked everything over. Ida drew a deep breath and followed. Here and there, lights flickered inside the wooden sleeper cars. She watched but didn't see anyone moving around inside. "Which one do you think the Wards are in?"

"They're probably home, sleeping in their own beds tonight," said Slick.

"Let's go, then," said Ida, short of breath.

Slick led the way back to the other side. He hunkered down and looked under the train, then swatted at a horsefly with his cap. His hair was all woolly instead of slicked down.

Safely in the open, Ida giggled. It felt so good, she laughed again.

"What're you looking at?"

"You," she said. "You should see your hair."

"You should talk."

"At least I combed mine."

Slick tugged his cap down tight and walked on past the lighted sections of train. He eyed each car carefully. "It'd be easy to leave town with them."

Startled, Ida said, "Why would you want to?"

"Why not? There's nothing keeping me here."

"Aunt Pliney."

"She's older than Moses."

"She looks after you, though."

"No, she doesn't. I look after her," said Slick. He

ducked into a pocket of darkness between train cars. "Come on."

"Huh-uh." Ida backed away. Wise to that trapped feeling, she wasn't crossing over again.

Slick scrambled up on a coupling. But this time he used it as a stepping-stone to a flatcar. He rolled under a bandwagon.

Watching him made Ida's stomach twitch. "What're you doing?"

"Just looking."

"You're going to get in trouble," she hissed. "I'm going!"

"With me?"

"No! Back!"

Slick leaped to the ground and overtook her in a couple of bounds. He dusted his hands together and hummed a circus song.

"You're not going with them," said Ida.

"Wanna bet? Bet me."

"I'm not betting, and you're not going."

Slick loped away, whistling in the dark. Watching, Ida scowled. He wasn't really going to do it. He was just talking big.

Chapter Sixteen

"Ida!"

Ida lifted her head and saw Vic jogging toward her.

"Mr. Beich says they're shorthanded at work. I told him I'd help out."

"But what about the circus?" cried Ida, stricken.

"General says you can go with him." Vic swung around and scanned the crowd watching the train unload. "I bumped into him a minute ago. He'll give you a ride home."

Ida soon found General. They watched the sun come up and the last wagon roll off the train, then followed the crowd to the nearby park. Roustabouts pounded stakes. Elephants pulled center poles into position. Tents mushroomed from the ground into a canvas city. Boys not much older than Ida carried water for the elephants.

"Let's go home for breakfast," said General, by and by.

"I've eaten," she said quickly.

"I haven't. Anyway, I promised Lizzy I'd be back in time for the parade."

"We're coming back, aren't we?"

"But, of course, magirl. It's circus day. Where else would we be?" he said, and nudged her toward the street.

* * *

Mom was coming down the fire escape when General stopped the wagon in the alley. Ida climbed down and ran to meet her on the stairs.

"Where's Vic?" asked Mom.

Ida explained about the change in plans. "General says I can go to the afternoon show with him and Aunt Lizzy. Do you want to come, too?"

"I'm going tonight," said Mom.

"You could tell Mr. Trainer you've changed your mind."

"But I haven't," said Mom. She smiled, then, and said, "How about if I watch the parade with you?"

They ate pancakes with Aunt Lizzy and General first. Then Mom broke her own rule and took Ida upstairs to the second floor. Mr. Wilson paused in cutting a fellow's hair to greet them. "The parade is about to start," he said. "There's still a little room left in the windows, if you want to watch it from here."

General and Aunt Lizzy accepted the barber's invitation and settled in to wait. But the little shop was hot and crowded, and Ida wanted a better view. It was strange about the circus. It was a public spectacle, meant for as many eyes as it could attract. Yet, to Ida, it was personal. She wanted to watch it without being watched. To close it up inside where she could take it out over and again and remember each sight and sound and smell and thrill. To feel it was *hers* in some way that it wasn't anyone else's.

"Come on," murmured Mom, leading the way into the corridor again. "I know a good place."

It was an unfurnished room cluttered with carpenter tools and ladders and a pile of lumber. The window was open.

Ida sat on the broad sill. Mom stood behind her as the first riders passed on the street below. Their bright flags and banners fluttered in the summer breeze. A man in a shiny buggy tipped his top hat to the crowds. Buglers followed on horseback. Their clear, rippling notes made Ida think of waterfalls.

She laughed at clowns in baggy trousers and big shoes and tapped her feet as the bandwagon passed. There were jungle critters in gilded cages, and more clowns on stilts and in pedal cars. There were fancy floats with singing wheels and ladies in spangles and gloves almost to their armpits. There were tumblers in tights and the Flying Wards! *Jennie! All in white! With feathers in her cap of short dark hair!*

"Jennie! Jennie! Up here!" Ida waved her arms and leaned so far out the window, Mom grabbed her skirt.

"Whoa, Ida," she cried in alarm.

Ida scarcely heard her over the roar in her ears and the cheering crowd. The Wards looked bigger than life! Like stars at the picture show, smiling and waving from their gilded float.

All too soon, they were gone. The elephants passed, tail to trunk to tail. The calliope came and went. "Cally-ope." That's how General said it. It wooed folks to the circus grounds with its throaty, reedy wail. But the excitement wasn't *really* over. The parade was only a taste of the real show, soon to begin.

"I'm going!" cried Ida. "Are you sure you won't come with us?"

"Ida, I'm going with Herman," Mom said quietly, as if to make the words stick.

The dark thoughts Ida had put away shifted closer. But Ida forced them back and hurried down the stairs. Aunt Lizzy huffed and puffed as General helped her up to the wagon seat. He gave Ida a hand, then climbed up after her and gathered the reins.

"Have a good time!" Mom called and waved.

The canvas city gleamed in the sunlight. There were children taking elephant rides on the grounds, and folks coming and going from the sideshow tent. There was a long line at the red ticket wagon. By the time Ida made it inside, the seats were crowded.

"It's a good crowd for the big show!" said General. His eyes glowed as they watched the "walk-around," in which all the performers paraded around the ring.

A man in a tall hat, black trousers, and a long-tailed black coat blew a whistle, and everyone paraded out again. The ringmaster, dressed all in red, announced the first act in flowery words. The show was under way.

Who taught bears to waltz and roller-skate and monkeys to drive a pony cart? How did mules know to roll barrels, and dogs to walk wires and teeter-totter and play Pick Up the Handkerchief?

There were leapers and tumblers and a tea party on a wire, and a man who scaled a pole that was balanced in the hands of a tiny lady in the ring eight feet below him.

"That's Gene and Mary Enos. They live here in Bloomington," said General.

The whistle blew. The applause was thunderous as the couple took their bows.

Ida longed to capture each act and to create from it a circus wall in her head. Her eyes couldn't move from ring to ring quickly enough to see it all. She laughed at the clowns' bungling pranks and cheered for a contortionist who folded himself into a small box and hid her face when the snake charmer handled the slithery reptiles.

There were aerial displays throughout the show, too. Solo acts, General called them. Some were done from ropes, others from revolving ladders, and some from trapezes. Ida studied each one carefully.

But the best was when the Flying Wards scaled to the top of the tent in the center ring. The band played flying music, and the sky was a maze of human bodies. Swinging. Leaping. Somersaulting with precision twists and passing one another in the air.

It was grand beyond description, and oh, so fleeting! Ida's eyes and ears and senses couldn't absorb it all, much less make room for the dingy thoughts Vic had dropped into her mind that morning. She cheered and clapped till her hands were numb and she felt a crushing loss when it was over.

When the departing audience had slowed to a trickle, General led the way down off the seats. Ida paused on the ground near the ring, dropped her head back, and gazed at the empty riggings. She closed her eyes and tried to keep the images from melting away like wet sugar.

"Come on, Ida darling," murmured Aunt Lizzy, urging her along.

Ida moved forward again, then stopped short, jaw dropping as a canvas curtain opened and Eddie Ward strode out. He was broad of chest and shoulders. His limbs were muscular. His hair was wavy. He wore it parted down the middle, like Slick's.

Ida's heart bumped as he stopped so close that she could have reached out and touched him.

"General! I thought that was you!" he said.

"This mug's hard to miss," replied General in his whispery voice, gripping Eddie's outstretched hand. "That was pure poetry, my boy. If I didn't know better, I'd say your troupe is part bird."

A grin darted across Eddie Ward's strong face. "How about that band? They can play the flyin' music, can't they?"

"Handily!" said General. He drew Aunt Lizzy to his side and introduced her to Eddie.

"Who's this? Your granddaughter?" asked Eddie, planting his hands on his hips as he looked at Ida.

"No. This is Ida Lou Young, a special friend and a keen admirer of the Flying Wards. Isn't that right, magirl?"

Ida bobbed her head and overcame her awe to say, "I'm going to be a trapeze girl someday."

"Then come see me when you're ready to join out, will you, kid?"

Ida's heart jumped to her throat as he reached for her hand. His grip was strong, his palm hard with calluses. Her hand tingled long after he had released it.

Eddie told General about some old riggings he wanted hauled off. General agreed and made arrangements to do the job. Aunt Lizzy nudged Ida out of the way of some propmen who were moving equipment, getting ready for the evening show.

"When are you going?" Ida asked General as Josephine trotted homeward beneath the pink-blue evening sky.

"Going where?"

"Out to Eddie Ward's barn."

"Monday morning," said General. "Why? Are you wanting to come along?"

"Could I?"

General chuckled. "You didn't think I'd go without you, did you, magirl?"

Ida hugged his arm. It gave her something new to look forward to, now that circus day was almost over.

"There's your mom and Mr. Trainer," said Aunt Lizzy, waving to an oncoming motorcar. "Is that Vic with them?"

"Looks like it," said General, tightening his grip on the lines.

Josephine was a steady horse. She plodded along, unperturbed by the passing motorcar. Ida wanted to be steady, too. But seeing the three of them together made her stomach feel the way her eyes did when she cut onions.

She thought of Dad, and of Vic's explanation of why what had once been would never be again. Ida fought the thoughts, chattering of all she had seen that day, until at last she was home.

"Thanks, General! Thanks, Aunt Lizzy," Ida cried as she jumped down from the wagon.

"Where are you going?" asked Aunt Lizzy.

"To get the circus bill off the side of the building!" Ida called back. She sprinted to the mouth of the alley, claimed the paper poster for her own, and raced upstairs to hang it on her circus wall.

But when she pulled the light string, her wall was not there.

Chapter Seventeen

The kitchen was wet with fresh plaster. Ida fled from the dull, damp, gray, coarse, nothing wall to the front room. Carpenters had been at work there, too. And in her bedroom. The walls were stripped down to bare lathes. She dropped to her knees and reached under the bed for her trapeze. *It wasn't there*.

Ida riffled through the clothes and blankets and trappings heaped on top of the bed. It wasn't with the draped furniture in the front room, either. Hands over her eyes, she tried to remember what she had done with it.

The kitchen! Last night. When Mr. Trainer told her there would be changes. She patted the top of the sheet-shrouded icebox. Peered under the stove. Scanned the pantry without success.

Had he thrown it away? He wouldn't dare! Would he? Ida flew to the empty landing and looked down on the scrap heap five stories below. The plumbing pipe, ripped from the walls, was there.

She stormed down the stairs and scattered tattered shreds of her circus wall, scrambling up the mountain of debris. She yanked the twisted water pipe out of the pile, looking. Scraped her hand on a nail as she dug deeper. Hissed and sucked her bloody palm. Blinked back hot tears. It was useless. Her wall was gone; her trapeze, too.

Ida thought of Slick going away. And of Eddie Ward. "... Come see me when you're ready to join out." She'd show Mr. Trainer what she thought of his changes, and Mom what she thought of Mr. Trainer, and Vic of his mean lies about Dad. She'd show them all!

Ida ran until she couldn't. Then she walked and caught her breath and ran some more. She reached the railway station with daylight to spare. The first section of the train was being loaded to make the jump to the next circus town. The rest would follow after the evening show.

The workmen's faces were shadowed by sweat-stained hats. Their shirts were wet, too. It was hard, hazardous work, winching the wagons up the runs and over empty flatcars. It left no time for watching out for children.

Ida looked, but Slick wasn't among the flock of people standing along the siding, watching. She eyed the empty flatcars in passing. How would she find him if he was already aboard, hiding?

I know! Ida sang her way past cage cars from the menagerie and tarp-covered wagons. Some were gilded with star-burst wheels. Others were plain work wagons, carrying tons of equipment. "Gilly wagons," General called them.

Ida reached enclosed cars and kept singing, listening for Slick to signal her in return. The enclosed cars were like baggage cars, only they wore the circus name in big, bright colors.

Maybe Slick was just talking big. Maybe he wasn't here.

Ida shooed the doubt away. She kept walking, kept looking, kept singing. She was almost to the end of the train when a catbird trilled. Only it wasn't a bird at all. Ida swung around to see Slick motioning to her from a patch of weeds growing along the siding. "If you're here to talk me out of going, forget it," he said as she ducked into the grass beside him.

"I'm not. I'm coming, too."

Slick's eyebrows arched. "Since when?"

"Eddie Ward said to see him when I'm ready to join out. I'm ready."

"He said *what*?"

"He did, Slick. He knows General." Ida told him about the riggings Eddie wanted hauled away, and how General had introduced her.

"He really said that? About you joining out, I mean?" Slick pressed.

"What do you think? That I made it up?" said Ida.

"If he wants you, then he'll take me for sure." Slick's gaze fell to her pockets. "Did you bring any eggs?"

"No."

"How about money?"

"I spent it all at the show."

"I'm broke, too." Slick patted his rumbling stomach. "Tomorrow, we'll be working for the circus. They'll feed us."

Ida's stomach churned, but it wasn't from hunger. She was eager to get on the train and go before . . . *before what?*

Ida let the thought go. She argued with Slick over

the best place to stow away. He wanted to hide under a wagon on a flatcar and ride in the open. The idea made Ida's stomach churn. "An enclosed car would be lots better."

"Doors are probably locked on them," said Slick.

They compromised. At dusk, Slick swung aboard a flatcar and pulled Ida up after him. They climbed the side of a gilly wagon and slipped under the tarp covering.

The wagon was full of canvas and cookhouse equipment. The tarp closed out the purple sky. It didn't leave much headroom. Ida lay on her stomach, drowning in canvas. Above her. Beneath her. Smelling it. Tasting it, as she buried her face in her arms.

She waited. Listened. At first, the bustling sounds in the yards crowded out the waving arms in her head. But the chuffing engine bumped hard as it hooked on. The jolt traveled the length of the coupled cars, and up her spine.

"We're moving!" whispered Slick. "Feel that?"

In every hair, ever cell, every bone. *Dear God*, prayed Ida, her heart banging. She hadn't been on a train in a long time. Not since Dad left.

But Mr. Trainer was *worse* than a train. He tore out her circus wall. And lost her trapeze. And Mom let him. That was the thing. *Mom let him.* Tears gathered. Ida blinked them back and clenched her jaw.

"Did you leave a note?"

"What?" said Ida, above the torrent of sharp, jagged thoughts.

"A note. Did you leave a note?"

"No."

"I did. But Aunt Pliney will forget as soon as she reads it. Or lose it. She's balmy."

Clackey-clack, over the track. Mouth dry, short-breathed, Ida made up a picture of Mom coming to see her in the big top. Mom by herself. Mom on her feet, cheering as Ida soared from the fly bar to the catch trap. Mom finding her after the show. Wet-eyed. Throwing glad arms around her.

"Come home, Ida. Please come home!" she'd plead. "I won't marry him, I promise."

But on the heels of that dream came an awful thought: Mom hadn't cried after Dad, or gone looking for him. *What if she doesn't look for me, either?*

Ida scrambled to the side of the wagon. She rose to her knees and butted the tarp with her head.

"You're rocking the boat!" yelped Slick. "Sit still."

"I can't breathe! I can't think!"

"Be quiet! Somebody'll hear!"

Ida didn't care. She wanted out. Wanted off. Wanted Mom. She clawed at the tarp, trying to make an opening.

"Stop it, Ida!"

"I want off!"

"*Now?* Are you crazy?"

"I'm not going! Help me, Slick! Help me!"

"If it ain't the canvas boss, it's kids!"

Ida's heart reeled as a hump she'd mistaken for canvas reared up in shadowy human form. Recoiling, she fell over Slick.

"Slick Baumgart, pleased to meet you, sir," said Slick, recovering. He shook himself free of her. "Tumbler, gymnast, and otherwise generally useful."

The man snorted. "You think it's all glitter and tinsel? Well, it ain't. There's blowdowns and washouts and fires, and snot-nosed runaways tramping over you when you're trying to sleep."

Ida forgot to breathe as the man yanked one corner of the tarp loose.

"You want off? You're off!" he said, and jerked her up and hurled her from the wagon.

Chapter Eighteen

Ida sailed clear of the lumbering train. A tangle of limbs broke her fall. Human ones. She lay in the cinders, clutching her hand and looking up at General, too stunned even to cry.

"By jingo, magirl, but you gave me a fright!" he exclaimed. "Are you all in one piece?"

Ida took stock and marveled that she was. Chin quivering, she asked, "What are you doing here?"

"Playing catch-net in your flying games, by the look of it," said General. He helped her to her feet, then motioned down track. "Better see about your friend."

Slick was picking himself up off the siding a few yards away. "Are you happy now?" he yelled over the noise of the moving train.

"Slick. I had to—"

"Chicken out, that's what! You're making work of this, I hope you know!" Slick turned toward the rails as if to make a second try.

"Whoa, my boy," called General, overtaking him. "Your aunt's counting on me to haul you home."

"She sent you?"

"I sent myself, with a detour by her house," said General. He caught Slick's arm and swung back toward the station. "Hurry every chance you get, or we'll be walking home. There wasn't time to tie Josephine, and she doesn't care much for trains."

"Ida, either. Spoiler!" said Slick, glowering at her. "I never should have told you I was going!"

Ida's nail-torn hand was bleeding again. She hugged it in her lap as Josephine clip-clopped down the lamp-lit street. They passed families gathered on porches and lawns and some at supper tables, beyond lighted windows. They looked happy, peaceful.

"Sorry" was on Ida's lips. She nudged Slick with her elbow. But he wouldn't talk, or even look at her. It made her think of the first time he'd come to Sunday school and she'd treated him the same way. She shouldn't have. It hurt on the receiving end.

Slick jumped to the ground in front of his aunt's house before Josephine was even stopped.

"Slick?" Ida tried one more time, wanting to make up.

But he walked up the path and closed the door without looking back.

Ida sneaked a glance at General. Ordinarily, he was a "live and let live" sort of fellow. But in coming after her, he'd broken his own code. She gripped her hurt hand and waited for him to scold her. But he didn't. "I'm sorry," she said finally.

General patted her knee and kept his eyes straight ahead. Ida swung her feet, anxious over what Mom would say, and sad over Dad. She was worn out as an old rag by the time General stopped the wagon behind the building.

"There you are! What do you mean, running off like

that?" Aunt Lizzy came up the basement steps, drying her hands on a dish towel.

"Easy with her hand, my pet. She's hurt," said General.

"Hurt?" exclaimed Aunt Lizzy. "Where? What happened?"

"I got gouged with a nail," sniffed Ida.

"Come inside and let Aunt Lizzy see."

Ida looked at General, wondering how much Aunt Lizzy knew. But General had his back to her, unhitching Josephine. She followed Aunt Lizzy inside.

"How'd you do this?" Aunt Lizzy asked as she bathed Ida's hand.

"On the junk pile."

"That dirty old thing?" Aunt Lizzy clucked her tongue. "Of all the places you could play."

"I wasn't playing." Ida swallowed the lump in her throat. Her eyes misted as she thought of her lost trapeze. "He threw it away."

"There, there," soothed Aunt Lizzy. "You're not making any sense. Who threw what away?"

"Mr. Trainer. He knocked down my circus wall, too."

Aunt Lizzy drew back in surprise. "Ida! You surely can't be mad at the man for trying to make things nicer for your mom?"

"He didn't even ask. He just knocked it to pieces and threw it out."

"But it leaked up there for years! By the time Mr. Summers fixed the roof, the walls were crumbling around you. Hold still, dear. I'm almost done."

Aunt Lizzy uncapped the iodine and painted Ida's wound. Ida hissed and blew. But it didn't sting as bad as her losses.

"Dad gave it to m-m-e. I was k-k-e-e-p-p-in' it, and now it's gone," she sobbed.

"Your *trapeze*? Is that what this is about?" exclaimed Aunt Lizzy. "For goodness' sake! It isn't gone. General found it on the pile. He put it up for safekeeping."

"Where?"

"If he said, I wasn't listening," replied Aunt Lizzy. "But somewhere safe, I'm sure. He'll be back from the livery in a moment, and you can ask him yourself. Now hold still and let me tie a bandage over this hand."

Ida dashed her tears and tried to stop crying. But the problem was bigger than an outgrown trapeze. Mr. Trainer's blunt words rang in her ears: "He s-s-a-a-i-d sit down and I s-s-a-t and he s-s-s-aid he's going to . . ."

Aunt Lizzy gathered her in her arms, patting and soothing. "Take a deep breath. Start over, now, and try it again. Slowly."

Ida told Aunt Lizzy everything, from Mr. Trainer's interest in marrying Mom right through her narrow escape from the train. All she left out was Vic's words about Dad. The ones she had closed away where they couldn't hurt her memories. Or her secret dreams about Dad coming back.

But Vic's words, tucked away, had risen like yeast left in the stove warmer. They were so big and loud, it was just the outside Ida getting chided and hugged and petted by Aunt Lizzy.

"Why, think of it! You could be speeding away on a train right this moment! Or worse," finished Aunt Lizzy with a shiver.

Ida heard General's feet on the rocks as he passed the basement window. She wiped her eyes. "Can I g-go see General about my trapeze?"

"Certainly. But you come right back. You're staying here tonight."

"What about Vic and Mom?"

"They're staying, too. Your beds are buried too deep to dig out," said Aunt Lizzy.

In household goods, she meant. Mom had stacked them out of the way of the carpenters. Ida didn't want to go upstairs, anyway. She wasn't ready to face that freshly plastered wall.

General was on the fire escape steps, unlacing his boots. Beside him was a basket of eggs. Mr. Trainer must have brought them when he came for Mom and Vic.

Ida sat down beside General. He tweaked her braid and whistled softly and held up an egg between his thumb and forefinger.

"Would you look at that, magirl? Eggs growing behind your ears!"

Ida held out her hand, then squeaked as he dropped the egg into it. The shell wasn't hard. It was just a soft membrane.

"Do you know what makes them that way?" asked General as Ida recovered her surprise.

"Not enough gravel in the hen," said Ida.

"You stole my thunder!" The smile in General's voice was like a hug. "Did your egg-begging friend teach you that?"

"No. My dad." Ida pressed her shoulder closer to his.

"Hmm."

Ida returned the egg to the basket on the steps. "Aunt Lizzy says you found my trapeze."

General reached under the steps. "Right here, magirl."

"It was there all the time?"

"Since this morning," said General.

"Thanks for finding it."

"That's why they call me Useful. What is it, Ida Loody?" he asked when she didn't respond. "You're not worried about your mama coming home and jerking a knot in your tail?"

"No. Dad *not* coming. Or coming, and being too late," admitted Ida.

General pulled off his boots, poked his laces inside, and didn't answer. The silence grew. Ida lifted her face. "General? What makes a dad go away?"

"You'd better ask your mama that one, magirl," General said quickly.

"I have. She never says. And Vic . . ." Ida couldn't make herself tell what Vic had said. She rolled the trapeze on her knees and wished she could roll Vic's words out so flat they'd disappear. Fresh tears burned her eyes. "I wish I knew what made him go, that's all."

General sighed. "What if I were to poke my patched nose where it doesn't belong and tell you to take a closer look at your sometimes-friend?"

"Who, Slick?"

"That's right."

"I didn't mean to make him mad," she said.

"Think about it, magirl. Even when you and Slick are getting along, who does he look after first?"

"Himself," said Ida.

"Exactly."

Ida waited, but General sat there silent as a period at the end of a sentence. Ida didn't see what Slick had to do with runaway dads. "I was talking about Dad," she said at length.

"I know. But sometimes-friends grow up looking after themselves first and others second. It's a hard habit to break, and a mistake when you don't."

Dimly, Ida sensed what he was saying. She wasn't sure he was right. He hadn't known Dad. He was trying to help, though. She picked at the rust on her trapeze. "I wish I'd known he was going. Maybe if I'd asked, he would have stayed."

"With sometimes-dads, the asking only delays the going, if that," said General gently.

Ida was quiet with her thoughts. At length, she asked, "Do you suppose he'll come back?"

"The road runs both ways, magirl. But it's uphill heading home, and some of us don't have enough gravel in our craws to make the climb."

Chapter Nineteen

General invited Ida to quilt with him while Aunt Lizzy prepared tomorrow's Sunday school lesson. But Ida's quilting hand wasn't up to it. She curled up on the circus trunk and cradled her bandaged hand. It ached.

"What if I get lockjaw?"

"Ida Lou! What a frightful thought!" exclaimed Aunt Lizzy.

"I wouldn't worry if I were you," said General. "It was a wall nail, wasn't it? How many carpenters do you know who have been stricken with lockjaw?"

Aunt Lizzy cleaned and medicated Ida's hand once more, just to be on the cautious side. Ida curled up again. The plucking of General's needle had lulled her to sleep when Mom slipped into the lamp-lit room and kissed her cheek.

Ida opened her eyes and tried to place the faint scent that lingered about her. "Where's Vic?"

"Herman said there was no reason for us to be crowding General and Lizzy when he has plenty of room. Vic's spending the night at his house." Mom smiled. "What did you think of the circus? Did you have a good time?"

"I liked it," said Ida, though after all that had happened, the show seemed as distant as the moon. "I met

Eddie Ward. Did General tell you? He said to come see him when I get ready to join out."

"She decided she was ready," said Aunt Lizzy. "Go on, Ida. Tell her about your misadventure. Confession is good for the soul."

It wasn't good for the eardrums. Mom lost her mellow mood in a hurry. She questioned and scolded and all but spouted flames. It was no more than Ida had expected. She cried and said she was sorry, and promised never to get on a train again.

"It isn't trains!" exclaimed Mom. "Don't you see, Ida Lou? Running away isn't the answer. That's the quitter's way. When you're scared or upset or angry or worried, you're to come to me and we'll talk about it."

"Even him?"

"Who?" asked Mom.

Ida knew how that edge in her voice could turn on a dime to "good riddance." "You're glad he's gone," she said in a whisper.

Mom's color deepened. She didn't deny it. Or discuss it. She, who had just said "come to me," forgot herself and ordered Ida to bed.

"I'll make up a spot for you on the floor," said Aunt Lizzy, the gentle hush after the storm. "General, open the trunk, please, and get out some quilts."

General retrieved a small key from his pocket. He started to unlock the trunk, then rose again, and dropped the key in Ida's hand. "You can make up your own bed, can't you, magirl? I believe I'll go for a short stroll before calling it a night."

Ida looked from the key to his scarred face and sunken eyes. "You mean I can look?"

"Yes, madear. It's time you did." He patted her shoulder, crossed to the door, and let himself out.

"I could use a cup of tea," said Aunt Lizzy to Mom. "Join me, won't you, Anna, and tell me all about your evening."

Mom followed Aunt Lizzy into the little kitchen, leaving Ida alone with the trunk. After all the times she had hinted and asked and dreamed of mysteries concealed inside, she was a heartbeat away from discovery. Visions of tinsel and glitter danced as she fit the key to the brass lock and lifted the lid.

A nine-patch quilt was on top. Beneath it was another quilt. And another. Five in all. Not at all what Ida had expected. Hoping for exciting things beneath, she made herself a bed on the floor beside the davenport where Mom would be sleeping and tiptoed back to the trunk.

"Ida? Are you bedded down?" called Mom from the kitchen.

"Just about," said Ida. Reassured by the silvery tinkle of spoons in teacups, she resumed her treasure hunt.

But it was disappointment upon disappointment. There were no whips. No posters of General, the tamer of wild jungle beasts. No tiger teeth or gawdy trinkets or tights or circus togs or braided bits of lion's mane. Not a single memento of General's days with the circus. It was all crocheted doilies, dish towels, aprons, pillowcases, dresser scarves, and other "fancywork" of Aunt Lizzy's making.

Ida sifted through retired sewing widgets at the bottom of the trunk and found a candy tin. Hope flickered afresh. Circus photo, perhaps? An old program, listing the displays? Or maybe a thin journal of scrawled memories? She removed the lid.

Inside were three old-fashioned pictures. The first was a tintype of a man in a Civil War uniform. General's father, perhaps? The next was of three curly-haired toddlers looking serious for the camera. The third was of a pretty young woman holding a baby in her lap. Ida jumped at a small sound, and looked up to see General returning from his walk.

There was no use pretending she hadn't been snooping. Caught red-handed, she turned the photograph his way. "Is this your mama?"

"No, madear. That's my first wife, Fanny, with little Eugenia. Poor girl wearied of the traveling life and took the wee ones home to her parents' farm."

Ida blinked, absorbing the meaning of his words. "You have children?"

"Four. Well grown, now, with little ones of their own."

Grandchildren! Ida's heart constricted at the realization there were other children in General's life. "How little?" she asked.

General's scarred face gathered into a wistful smile. "I really couldn't say. I don't see much of them."

Ida wondered why that was. But it relieved her of having to worry about sharing General. It was troubling enough to know he had a whole life she knew nothing about.

Ida looked at the tintype and the two photographs again, then put everything back where she had found it and returned the key to General. He tucked it into his pocket and patted her on the head. "Good night, magirl. This old lion tamer's turning in."

Ida bid him good night and watched the bedroom door close behind him. She stretched out on the quilt-padded floor. Slick flitted to mind. Dad, too. General's mention of uphill climbs. And finally, when Mom came in from the kitchen, a delayed recognition of that scent Ida had caught just before the storm.

It was like Mr. Wilson's barbershop. Hair tonic. Shaving cologne. It was the scent of Mr. Trainer. Ida pressed her lips together as she thought of Vic staying the night at his house. The heat of her earlier rebellion flickered.

"Did you have a nice time with Mr. Trainer?" Ida asked as the lamp winked out at Mom's touch.

"Yes," said Mom.

"He knocked out my circus wall."

There was silence. Ida had neglected to take off her dress. In her pocket was a scrap of eggshell. She turned it in her fingers. "What about Dad?"

The davenport springs creaked as Mom turned. "What about him?"

"He might come back."

"He won't."

"You don't know that," said Ida.

Mom sighed. She rose on an elbow and found Ida's hand in the darkness.

"Could you ask him to?" pressed Ida.

"Come back?" asked Mom. "No."

The jagged edge of shell pricked like tears behind tired eyelids. Ida asked, "Why not?"

"He made a new life for himself. It was his decision, and now it's too late."

A life with someone else? Ida couldn't repeat what Vic had said. A light on it would make it real. If Mom said it was so, it couldn't be erased. If she said it wasn't so, what was true and what was protection?

"Is he mad at us?" she asked finally.

"At you? No," said Mom. "Of course not. He was proud of you and Vic. Miles and years won't change his feelings for you."

Ida brushed the shell from her fingertip. She sat up and leaned against the bottom of the sofa. Mom stroked her hair. "Why doesn't he come see us?" she asked.

"He's too far away, Ida."

"How do you know?"

"He wrote, once."

"When?"

"Shortly after he left."

"How come you never told me? Where's the letter?"

"I threw it away."

"But, why?" asked Ida, stricken.

"The letter was to me. It wasn't for a child's eyes." Into the silence, Mom added, "And because I was angry."

"You still are," said Ida.

"Yes," said Mom quietly. "I'm sorry if it's touched you."

"It hasn't," said Ida.

"Lizzy says it has." Mom slipped to the floor and stretched out on the quilts Ida had spread. "I can't sleep on that sofa. You're welcome to it."

But Ida didn't want the sofa. She wanted her mother. She curled up beside her. The faint scent that reminded her of fathers brought the sting of more tears. They dripped on Aunt Lizzy's quilt, for she was too tired to wipe them away.

Chapter Twenty

Slick wasn't in Sunday school the next morning. It was his first miss since the rainy morning he had showed his face at the window and Aunt Lizzy invited him in.

Aunt Lizzy worried over him on the walk home. "I hope he isn't sick."

"He was fine yesterday," said Ida, skipping along between Aunt Lizzy and Mom.

"Perhaps we should call at his aunt's house," said Aunt Lizzy.

"Do you know her?" asked Mom.

"No. But General does. He could hitch up the horse after lunch."

"Slick will show up. He always does," said Mom.

"He's mad at me. That's why he didn't come," said Ida.

Whenever they quarreled, he was quick to make up. Mom was right. He'd show up. If not today, then soon.

Vic and General were upstairs with Mr. Trainer and a couple of carpenters when Ida arrived home. Mr. Trainer had coaxed the men into giving up their day off so they could push out a wall and make room for an indoor toilet and sink and bathtub. The rush was on to get the room framed up, the plumbing roughed in. The plasterers would return tomorrow.

Ordinarily, Mom frowned on Sabbath breaking. But she was beholden to Mr. Trainer for his helpfulness and indebted to General and Aunt Lizzy for their hospitality.

"I hope we'll be back upstairs and out of your way by midweek," Ida heard Mom say as they helped Aunt Lizzy spread a noonday meal.

Ida wasn't in any hurry. Seeing fresh plaster where her circus wall used to be was too tender a bruise. Besides, she liked staying with Aunt Lizzy and General.

When dinner was ready, Ida and General took their plates out on the fire escape to make room at the table for Mr. Trainer and the carpenters. Aunt Lizzy soon joined them there. Slick's name came up as they were eating.

"I'm worried about the boy," admitted Aunt Lizzy. "You don't think he—"

"Took off again?" General finished for her. "Perhaps. All he had to do was slip back to the station and stow away on the second section of train."

Had he? Ida's heart thudded. *Spoiler*, she heard the word again. He had wanted to go. Badly.

Aunt Lizzy's frown deepened. "If you saw it coming, you should have taken measures to prevent him."

"How, my pet? Short of tying him up."

"What kind of a home does he have that he's so anxious to run away?"

"His home isn't the problem, Lizzy," said General. "It's his father that's worrying Slick. He's in some trouble."

"He's in jail," Ida spoke up.

General's brow contracted. "And about to get deported, by the sound of it."

"Kicked out of the country?" Aunt Lizzy's hand flew to her throat. "Oh, dear heaven! Don't tell me he's a sp—"

"A what? What is he? Tell me!"

"Ida, darling. We're living in troubled times," hedged Aunt Lizzy. "This is a grown-up matter."

"Mr. Baumgart is German, Ida," General's voice ran like a quiet current. "He's got family in the old country. He's been charged with being against the war. He will go to trial soon."

"Is he guilty?" asked Ida.

"Maybe," said General. "Or maybe he's one hundred percent American in his sentiments and folks have misunderstood him. Whichever it is, you can see how Slick might think the grass is greener on the circus lot."

Ida gripped her plate with her good hand. "You mean Slick will get kicked out of the country if his dad does?"

"I'm not saying one thing or the other. I'm not sure Slick knows the answer himself. But he does know they can't ship what they can't find," said General.

Understanding flooded in. No wonder Slick was so upset with her! *Spoiler, spoiler,* the word rang again. Heat flooded her face. "I hope he *did* go."

"Ida, darling, you don't know what you're saying!"

"I wouldn't worry, madear," soothed General. "Slick's pretty good at landing on his feet."

"He's just a boy!" countered Aunt Lizzy. "He needs his family."

"He'll find one with the circus," said General.

"Did you?" she challenged.

General's scarred face twitched. "I didn't get all

scratched up without learning there are some cats you don't tangle with. Slick's a bright boy. He'll learn, too."

Ida helped with the dishes. There were a lot of them. The water was turned off upstairs so the men could rough in the plumbing. Mom and Aunt Lizzy sent her upstairs with drinking water for them.

"Get the syrup while you're up there, Ida, and the popcorn, and we'll make popcorn balls," said Mom.

The hot, thirsty men thanked Ida for the bucket of water. Out of breath from the five-story climb, she found the popcorn and syrup, plunked down on the top step to rest, and set the popcorn and syrup down, too. The syrup bottle wobbled and rolled. Lunging for it, Ida fell against the brace that supported the paint-bare handrail.

There was no warning. Just the sound of splintering wood and her own scream as she hurtled through space.

Chapter Twenty-one

"I've got you, my pet."

General's hoarse whisper broke through the airless black fog that enveloped Ida even before she hit the ground. At his touch, the breath rushed into her lungs again. Pain shot up her arms and legs and back as he lifted her from the scrap heap that had once been her circus wall.

"Hold on, baby! Hold on!" sobbed Mom.

To what? Dark cotton waves lapped over Ida. They were fluffy and thick, like clouds. Mom's cries got lost in them. Aunt Lizzy's, too.

When Ida awoke, someone was hammering her legs. She thought it was Slick, pretending to be a doctor. She screamed and tried to kick, but Mom and Aunt Lizzy held her down. General's scarred face was wet with tears. Vic was there. And Mr. Trainer. She could smell his hair tonic.

What a low-down, sneaky trick, nailing her legs to the bed.

Ida awoke to see a woman holding a cup to her lips, urging her to drink. She was wearing a white apron on her head and pretending to be a nurse. But Ida wasn't fooled. She had played that game herself.

* * *

Mom was on her knees, mopping the floor with Oil of Gladness. Or was she praying? The room swam. What was wrong with her woozy head? The words Ida wanted would not come. Why couldn't she talk? Lockjaw? Was that it? Did she have lockjaw?

No. It wasn't lockjaw. Her jaws worked. Ida opened her mouth one morning and talked. But when words hit the air, the sound wasn't right. She was confused. Peppery inside. Cross at being tricked. And certain that Slick was behind it somehow.

The nurse was real. And the hospital. Ida's legs were broken, and her right arm, too. She knew because Vic told her, and General said it was true. He came with Aunt Lizzy. They hugged and patted and were so gentle and weepy, Ida thought someone had died.

Mr. Trainer came. He sat at Ida's bedside and talked to Mom. His voice was hushed. Chuff-chuff-chuff. Like a train, idling on the tracks. What was that he slipped on Mom's finger? It glittered like buried treasure from the war garden.

Ida asked Mom to read about Jennie Ward's fall from the top of the circus tent. She wanted the secret to getting well. Mom said her circus wall was gone. Ida cried and wanted it back. Mom said why didn't she make a scrapbook instead? Then she showed Ida the broken glass on her finger. She said she was getting married. Ida didn't understand. Wasn't she married to Dad? The divorce, said Mom, was final. Ida tried to remember what the word meant.

Ida took a trip by motorcar. When she woke up, she was in a strange bed. It was dark wood. There was a hunting scene carved on the tall headboard. It wasn't her bed. But she couldn't get out of it. She tried, because she needed to close the door so Mr. Trainer wouldn't see her. She was off-limits. If he caught her in his house, she would have to run like a deer.

The lathes and plaster pile that had broken Ida's fall had riddled her with nail punctures. Weeks of careful nursing cleared up her infections. The swelling in her head went down, and her confusion faded. She remembered what divorce meant, and knew that Mr. Trainer was her stepfather now. She was living in his house.

General and Aunt Lizzy came to visit her every Sunday afternoon. But it wasn't the same as being neighbors. Ida missed her circus wall. She missed her friends from school, and walking the curb on the square. Most of all, she missed Slick. "Why doesn't Slick come see me?"

"He ran away with the circus, remember?" said Mom.

Of course! And she had, too. Or started to. Only she'd changed her mind. "Maybe he'll be home in the fall. Do you think?"

Mom blinked back tears and kissed her cheek. "Drink your milk, Ida Lou. It's good for your bones."

Ida's corner room with its big windows and dark, heavy drapes and velvety-looking wallpaper was handsome. There was a framed map of the United States on the wall that she did not like. It pictured railroad lines crisscrossing the country. It looked like long lazy stitches on a not-very-pretty quilt.

"This was Herman's den, and will be again, once you can climb the stairs," Mom explained, and hung a print of girls and dogs beside the map.

Shelves of dull-looking books stood straight as soldiers beside the new books Mom had bought for Ida. The books had pretty covers. But Ida had no more interest in them than she had in the carved wooden ducks that shared shelf space with the painted china dolls. Mom said Herman had carved the ducks himself. The dolls, she said, had belonged to his mother. They were pretty to look at, but hard to keep dusted. Not that Mom had to worry about that. Two young women did the dusting. They filled Ida's water pitcher, too. And swept and polished and giggled about Mr. Trainer and his new bride as if Ida's ears were broken along with the rest of her.

Ida's arm healed. She could feed herself again, but summer was gone before the bones in her legs mended. They were scarred and spindly and weak and ugly. They wouldn't hold her up. She was afraid she would never walk again.

Mr. Trainer said she needed exercise. He drove iron hooks into the ceiling over the foot of her bed and attached pulleys to the hooks, and cables to the pulleys. Mom elevated Ida's lower legs on soft pillows, then lifted her legs so that her knees were bent. Her upper legs, from hips to knees, were vertical to the bed.

Mr. Trainer buckled leather straps around Ida's lower legs and fastened them to the cables. He used the pulleys to lift one leg, then the other. It hurt. Ida cried for him to stop.

"You want to walk, don't you?"

Ida wept and said that she did.

"Very well, then. Get a stiff upper lip and let's continue."

He adjusted the weight on the pulleys, then exercised her legs some more. It reminded Ida of circus men winching wagons up on flatcars. And of Slick. Sometimes-friends didn't visit people who couldn't walk. When she walked, she would go see him and tell him what she thought of sometimes-friends. She held tight to Mom's hand and didn't cry out again.

Night came. Ida dreamed she was Jennie Ward, soaring from the fly bar and missing the catch. She didn't hit, though. She woke up, first. Or maybe she blacked out from the air whooshing out of her lungs the way it had when she fell from the fire escape.

It was the first of many exercise sessions, and many dreams about falling. After a while, Ida welcomed the dreams. In them, for a fraction of a moment, she was the old Ida. Moving freely, and without any pain.

Sometimes, Ida dreamed about Slick looking for her. She hid from him, not wanting him to see her until her legs worked again.

"Herman would like for you to join us for dinner," said Mom one autumn day after Ida's exercise treatment. "Rest awhile, then Vic will be in to carry you to the table."

"I'm too tired," she said when Vic came to get her.

Vic came again the next morning. And at suppertime, too. Every time Mom or Mr. Trainer sent him to get her, Ida refused to go.

After a few days, Vic lost his temper. "Stop being a pain and come to the table!"

"Let it go, Vic," said Mr. Trainer from the open door. "She'll come when she's ready."

"What're you sulking about, anyway?" asked Vic when they were alone.

"I'm not."

"Then what's the matter? How hard can it be, getting carried to the table?"

"I don't want to be carried anywhere," said Ida.

"You beat all, you know that?" Vic left in a huff.

Vic was out of the candy factory and back in school. Mr. Trainer liked Vic. He talked to him about school and business and politics. Mr. Trainer liked politics. He was thinking of running for mayor. But he didn't speak of this to Ida. All he talked about to her was her exercises.

Ida turned on her side and watched the wind rough the trees beyond her window. Leaves drifted and blew away faster than she could count them. Like her losses.

Dad. Home. Her health. Her mobility. A whole summer, and now autumn, too. She missed her friends. She even missed school. Most of all, she missed Slick, and wondered about his father and if the deporters deported him. She asked. Mr. Trainer said no, that the evidence against Mr. Baumgart was insufficient. The court had released him from jail some months ago. He had gone to Indiana.

How would Slick find his father in Indiana? she asked. Mr. Trainer didn't know. Mom kissed her cheek and left it damp, and reached for her sewing basket. She threaded a needle for herself and another for Ida, and asked for her help with the quilt she was making. It was an Underground Railroad quilt like the one Dad had taken when he went away. Ida stitched a few pieces together, and fell asleep with the needle and cloth in hand.

General and Aunt Lizzy came for their Sunday visit. One of the young women who cleaned brought them to Ida's room while she was doing her exercises. General scattered a handful of autumn leaves over her bed.

The crisp, clean scent of them made Ida want to be outdoors. "Take me outside, would you, General? Please?"

"Outside?" cried Mom. "When you haven't even been out of your room? Don't be silly!"

"Let's finish up here, Ida," said Mr. Trainer over Mom's objections. "If you feel up to being moved, you can join us in the front parlor."

Mom ushered General and Aunt Lizzy into the parlor to wait, then returned to hold Ida's hand. The session was long and hard, and the sheets itched, and the smell of Mr. Trainer's hair tonic was heavy in the air.

"Can't we stop?" begged Ida. "General'll get tired of waiting."

Mr. Trainer took out his pocket watch. "One more minute and we'll have it for the day."

Ida burst into tears. But he finished the full minute, anyway, then left her with Mom.

"I know it hurts, Ida," said Mom. "But don't take it out on Herman. He is doing his best."

"Him and his junky old fire escape. It's his fault!"

"No, it isn't, and you aren't to say that. He would be hurt if he knew you thought it," warned Mom.

And she should care about that? *She* was the hurt one.

"It was an accident," said Mom, her voice low. "He feels terrible about it. He's doing all he can to help you walk again."

"You're on his side."

"There are no sides. Dry your eyes, and I'll get General."

Mom left in a swish of silk and perfume. Ida flung a pillow at Mr. Trainer's train map just as the door opened. Her nerves jumped. But it was only General.

"Someone call for a lion tamer?" He dropped a parcel into a chair and picked up the pillow.

Ida's chin quivered. "Where's Aunt Lizzy?"

"Drinking tea with your mother."

Ida dried her eyes on the sheet. "Unbuckle me, would you? Mom forgot."

"This is quite a riggin'."

"It isn't a rigging, it's a hateful old torture machine," muttered Ida as General freed her legs of the straps.

"What's the matter, magirl? Feeling soft-shelled?"

Ida shredded a leaf and brushed it off on the floor. "Is the circus season over yet?" she asked, still thinking of Slick.

"Yes. Those who winter here are trickling home. I watched a few acts practice yesterday at the Y."

"Was Slick there?"

"At the Y?" he said, and dropped his gaze. "No."

"What about the Wards?"

He shook his head.

Ida picked at the ivory tatting on the edge of the sheet. "You know how Jennie missed her trick and fell from the top of the circus tent that time? The story was on my circus wall. Remember?"

"As if it were yesterday."

"I dream about it sometimes. Only it's me in her skin."

General stood up and crossed to the window. He stood motionless, his hands in his pockets, his shoulders bunched. When he turned to face the bed again, his face was wet.

"What is it?" asked Ida, alarmed.

"It's Jennie, magirl," he said gently. "It's time someone told you. Jennie Ward is dead."

Chapter Twenty-two

Dead. The word entered Ida's ears, shivered through her body, and kept echoing. General wiped his patched face, watching, waiting.

"Did she fall?" Ida asked finally.

"No," said General. "An empty troop train slammed into the circus train. It plowed through the caboose and into bunker cars where folks were sleeping. Jennie was killed instantly. Another girl, too."

"Eddie?"

"Not Eddie. He freed himself and his flying troupe, too." General's throat worked. His chin quivered as he struggled to go on. "He got all of his people out, then moved on to the other wooden sleepers as the wreckage went up in flames. But for many, it was too late."

Ida knew without him saying it that General had lost friends. Tears slid down her face and dripped on her hand. "When?" she whispered.

"In June. Just after your fall."

Suddenly, horribly, Ida feared there was more. "Was Slick—"

"I don't know," he said.

"But his father—"

"By the time Mr. Baumgart was tried and released and went to see about the boy, the trail was cold."

"What about Aunt Pliney?"

"She hasn't had any word of him."

Ida clutched the sheet so tight, her knuckles turned white. Slick couldn't be dead. If he were, someone would know. There would be a grave, and a column in the paper.

"Seventy people died in the blazing wreckage, magirl," said General brokenly. "Some bodies were never identified."

General left Ida staring at the contraption he had called a rigging. She couldn't think about Slick. Not yet. The shock was too raw. She stared at the thing and tried to pretend that it *was* a rigging. And that she was swinging from the fly bar and somersaulting through the air. Like Jennie.

But she wasn't like Jennie. Or Slick. They were daring, and she wasn't. She had lost her courage months ago. That's why they'd waited so long to tell her about Slick and about Jennie. They had been afraid to tell her.

Ida inched her upper body up and up and hooked her hands behind one knee to take the pressure off her bed-weary back. Her knee wouldn't come to her chest. Not even halfway.

Her legs would barely bend. Barely. "Barely" was a squeak-by word. It was close to flat on your back and a far cry from "ta-da." But it wasn't dead and buried. Poor Slick. Poor Jennie.

Mom came in. The goose-down mattress gave as she sat down and took Ida's hand. "Are you all right?"

Ida's throat swelled. "I hate trains."

"I know," murmured Mom.

She was wearing a new dress. It was blue, with a gold pin on the milky white collar. Her hair was piled on her head like an auburn cloud, and she smelled nice. But all that add-on softness couldn't hide lines in her careworn face as she leaned close and kissed Ida's cheek.

"General brought you something earlier," she said, and crossed to the chair where General had dropped the parcel. "He asked me to give it to you."

Ida fought back scared, sad, lonesome, angry tears. She pulled the string and peeled back the plain brown wrappings. The Ohio Star quilt. The one they had quilted for the Red Cross Liberty Auction. She ran her hands over the stars and black-and-white polka-dot sashings.

Her eyes filled. Her senses, too, with pluck-plucking needles and whispery thread. Swinging feet from General's circus trunk. Wrapped snug in jackpot and laughter while green beans bubbled on Aunt Lizzy's stove. Potluck plates on the shady fire escape. Racing and chasing until the sun sank on Yank and nurse games and the courthouse clock rang the hour. It seemed so long ago.

"General made the highest bid at the Liberty Auction," said Mom, though Ida hadn't asked.

Ida lifted her gaze, a wordless "why?"

"Because you're his pet," said Mom brokenly.

Crisp colors blurred together as Ida ran her fingers over the pieces. Stars. A message of light. A message of love. Like General's face. Who would think that scars could be beautiful like stars?

Mom leaned close and kissed her cheek. "Could you eat some supper?"

Ida wiped her eyes. She was so tired of this room and this bed and holding fear close so no one else would see it. She couldn't bear to be alone with thoughts of Slick and Jennie. She hugged the quilt tight and choked back tears. "Send Vic for me. I want to eat at the table."

Chapter Twenty-three

The guns were silenced. The war was won! The Yanks were coming home. On Armistice Day, Ida took her first wobbly steps. Sandwiched between Mom and Vic, she made it to the parlor window.

There was a park across the street. It was the size of a city block. Neighborhood boys had built a bonfire around an effigy of Kaiser Bill. His tyranny went up in flames. Bells rang. Women beat pans. Children waved flags. Grown men shot off fireworks while young men raced horses around the square. And the singing! Listening to the joy in their voices gave Ida goose bumps. She begged to go out. But the air was cold, influenza was raging, and Mom was sure all the excitement wasn't good for her.

The next day was sunny and warm for November. Mr. Trainer carried Ida out to the veranda. Mom tucked her Ohio Star quilt around her. In the park across the street, children kicked through the cinders of yesterday's fire and raced through piles of leaves. Ida watched, wishing they'd come over. It had been so long since she'd had friends to talk to, and share secrets and play with. But the children seemed not to notice her there on the porch.

It was a handsome neighborhood. The houses were two and three stories tall, no two alike. Some were of brick, some wood-frame. They had interesting details, the names of which Mr. Trainer told her as he whittled on a chunk of wood.

Ida watched the pile of shavings grow and saw that it would be another duck. He stood up and stretched and took out his gold pocket watch. "I'll take you inside, Ida. I have business to attend to at the bank."

"Are we rich?" asked Ida.

Mr. Trainer crooked a rusty eyebrow. "It's 'we' now, is it?" he said as he carried her inside.

"Are *you?*" Ida rephrased her question.

"It isn't polite to ask," he said.

He corrected her manners now that her health was improving. Her grammar, too. It annoyed Ida. She paid him back with "ain'ts" and "done dids" and, that night, at the dinner table, she belched. On purpose.

Mom chided, and Vic got mad. He carried her back to her room, dumped her in a chair, and told her it wasn't right to enjoy the house and food and the clothes Mr. Trainer put on her back, then think she couldn't be corrected.

"It isn't his place, he isn't my dad," Ida replied without much heat. "And neither are you."

"Who'd want to be?" Vic said, and slammed her door on his way out.

The ceiling didn't fall. Not even a speck of dust. But the words hurt Ida's feelings. Later, she listened as Mr. Trainer helped Vic with his homework, and wished she had homework, too.

* * *

General and Aunt Lizzy came on Sunday afternoon. Ida made it to the parlor, using Vic and a cane.

"Watch this!" she said, and struck a wobbly pose.

"In center ring, the enchanting Ida Loody," said General as Aunt Lizzy enveloped her in a powdery hug.

"Can I play in the leaves now?" asked Ida.

"Oh, Ida! I don't think so," began Mom.

"You can't hover over her forever, Anna," said Mr. Trainer. "Wrap her up, and I'll help her out. And that's 'may I,' Ida."

Ida crowded down her resistance and said, "May I?"

"Yes, you may."

Mr. Trainer got on one side, General on the other. They eased Ida down on the wicker veranda chair. Then Mr. Trainer got rakes from the carriage house. He and General and Aunt Lizzy and Mom soon had a huge pile of leaves gathered on the lawn.

Mom brought a buggy robe from the house. She spread it over the leaves. But Ida didn't stay on the robe. She rolled in the leaves and threw them in the air and watched them float in graceful spirals. Like circus girls.

The sharp air stung her nose and cheeks. Mom hovered close and tried to talk her into returning indoors. Ida pleaded for five more minutes. Reluctantly, Mom agreed and returned with the grown-ups to the veranda for tea.

Ida turned the rake upside down and planted it on the ground. She wrapped her hands around it and was pulling herself to a standing position when a dog streaked across the yard. Mom yelled a warning and jumped up so fast, she upset her tea.

Ida squealed and braced herself. But the dog dodged at the last moment. He raced in circles, a blur of cinnamon fur, yipping and wiggling and wagging his crooked tail.

"Wags!" cried Ida, recognizing him. She let go of the rake and tumbled into the leaves, crying, "Where'd you come from?"

As Ida hugged him, the dog's young master raced across the yard, yelling, "Swisher! Get down!"

Wags rolled out of Ida's arms and dropped to his haunches.

"Hey!" cried the red-haired boy, stopping short. "It's you! You're the girl who found Swisher last summer."

"I remember," said Ida. Wanting up from the ground, she stretched out a hand. But before the boy could take it, Swisher put his paw in it. She giggled. "He's smart!"

"I trained him myself," said the boy, beaming. "Watch this! Swisher! Swisher! Speak!"

"Roofff!" barked Swisher.

"Bravo!" Ida clapped and cheered for the dog.

Mr. Trainer hurried across the yard and helped Ida to her feet. "What have I told you about that dog, Alvin?"

"Sorry, sir." Alvin stooped to catch Swisher by the collar.

"Oh, don't!" cried Ida, seeing his intentions. "He's glad to see me, he wants to play."

"He knocked you down!"

"No, he didn't. I fell all by myself. Can't he stay? Please?"

"I don't know," said Mr. Trainer, brow furrowing. "Can you keep him in check, Alvin?"

"Yes, sir. He minds very well. Sit, Swisher. Stay!" He lifted his face. "See?"

"Would you join us for tea?" called Mom from the porch.

"I don't care for any, thank you," said Alvin.

"What about cookies and circus stories?" said Ida as General came across the yard. "Do you like either one of them?"

"Both," said Alvin, nodding.

"Me, too. This here's General, and he's a lion tamer."

"That's 'May I introduce you to . . . ,' Ida," Mr. Trainer began.

"We've already met, sir," said Alvin, politely.

General laughed his whispery laugh, and shook Alvin's hand. Mr. Trainer permitted himself a small smile, and gave up correcting children for the day.

Chapter Twenty-four

Once the flu epidemic was over, Ida coaxed Mom into inviting Alvin and his sisters to come play games with her on their way home from school. The girls, of which there were seven in all, often had music or dance or art lessons. But Alvin came without fail. He was a year younger than Ida, courteous and fair.

"He has the sunniest disposition I've ever seen in a boy," declared Mom with hearty approval.

Alvin also had a passion for animals, and a lot of pets. Besides Swisher, there was Tory the crow, Mandy the parlor cat, Pretty Boy Pony, a goat named Three-Foot Grump, and a green snake that Ida asked him to please never let loose in their parlor again.

Alvin's two oldest sisters got married in a double wedding just after Christmas. But Alvin and the remaining five spent the winter revitalizing Ida with their lively company. By spring, she was accompanying them to her new school. Mr. Trainer's home was in a different ward than their apartment had been. But despite Ida's efforts, she was so far behind in her studies that her teacher said she would have to repeat fifth grade.

"Nonsense! With a little extra effort, you can catch up," said Mr. Trainer when Ida limped home to cry on

Mom's shoulder. "I'll speak to the principal about help-ing you over the summer."

True to his word, Mr. Trainer got Ida's books from school and tutored her. While the children's voices rang in the park across the street, he drilled her in long divi-sion and history and other subjects, dull as dirt. They were a trial to each other. But his stuffy, exacting meth-ods paid off. Ida passed her exams when school resumed, and moved ahead with her class.

With Ida's academic crisis solved, Mr. Trainer, a city alderman for years, turned his attention to running for mayor. He was busy hatching strategies. He didn't notice when Ida's abandoned exercise contraption dis-appeared from the storage closet under the stairs.

In the carriage house was a loft where hay used to be kept. It extended over half of the carriage house. The other half, where Mr. Trainer parked his motorcar of an evening, was open all the way to the roof. It was in the loft that Ida, Alvin, and his sisters spent a rainy Saturday morning taking the contraption apart. They stopped for lunch, then regrouped to hang the pulley part of the contraption from an overhead beam. Alvin was the only one good enough with tools to secure the pulley so that there was no danger of it falling. He had to work from a ladder propped on a wide board that stretched between two beams. Alvin, like his dog, did not like heights. He was wobbly-kneed and wet as a mop by the time he climbed down again.

"You did good, Alvin," said Ida. "I'll do the rest."

Ida climbed the ladder and threaded a long rope

through the pulley. She threw one end down to Alvin on the floor below. Alvin's sisters in the loft caught the other end. Ida moved the ladder out of the way, then joined Alvin on the dirt floor and tied a loop in that end of the rope.

"You worked the hardest. Do you want to try it out first?" she asked.

"No, you can," said Alvin. He scaled nailed slats to the half-loft, where his sisters waited with their end of the rope.

Ida sat in the loop and wrapped her hands around the rope.

"Ready?"

"Ready!" Ida called back.

Alvin and his sisters pulled, towing Ida aloft. Then, on the count of three, they jumped out of the loft into a pile of dusty straw below. The weight of their descent sent Ida shooting toward the rafters in her loop swing.

"Whee!" she cried, and looked down to see Alvin's sisters clinging to the rope like flies on a gum strip. Alvin had not jumped. He was still in the loft. But his weight was not missed. It had been a splendid ride.

"I'm next! I'm next!" Ida's anchors clamored for the next turn as they lowered Ida to the floor.

"It's Alvin's turn," said Ida. "Come on, Alvin. It's fun."

"No thank you," he said.

His sisters, each in turn, tried to coax Alvin into giving it a try. He would not be persuaded. Not then. And not in the coming days, at the end of the school day when they all hurried home to play.

Mom didn't pay much heed to the straw Ida was dragging in on her after-school clothes, or to how much time she was spending in the carriage house. She had more important things to think about. She was having a dinner party for Mr. Trainer's political supporters. It was all new to her, and she was stuck on after-dinner entertainment.

"Whatever you decide will be fine, Anna," said Mr. Trainer when she consulted him.

"Alvin's sisters could play music," suggested Ida.

"Hmm," said Mom.

Ida followed her into the parlor and did an egg-stand on the sofa. "Their cat sings," she said from her upside-down position.

"That's nice," said Mom.

"Mom? Can we have matching dresses?" Ida had developed a fondness for pretty dresses. Even the scraps proved useful. With Mom's help she was crazy-quilting them together, learning new stitches. Circus girls needed skill with a needle so they could make pretty costumes.

"You won't need a dress; it's a grown-up party, Ida," said Mom.

But Ida, off on a flight of fancy, wasn't listening. "I know! We'll make a Maypole. I'll dance around it while Alvin's sisters play. You can dance, too. We'll look good in our matching dresses. Except it isn't May."

"Who isn't May?" said Mom. The distracted look in her eye faded as she noted Ida's egg-stand on the sofa. "Would you sit up right? Your bloomers are showing."

Poor Mom. She wasn't cut out for parties. It was

making her so nervous, she was eating too much. Her dresses were getting tight. Ida stood up and smoothed her skirt down and crossed to the desk to look over Mom's shoulder. "New dress" wasn't on her list.

Ida sighed and went out to the carriage house. Alvin and his sisters soon joined her. She explained Mom's problem, and her idea about music. Alvin's sisters were pleased to have their talent noticed and were eager to be on the entertainment committee.

"I want to dance, too," said one of the girls.

"I recite poetry," said another modestly.

"Three-Foot Grump eats tin cans," said Alvin. "She bows, too. When she's in a good mood."

"And butts when she isn't."

They all giggled as Alvin's youngest sister rubbed her fanny.

"Ida's mom is having a dinner party, not a three-ring circus," inserted an elder sister, the best musician among them.

Ida's blinked and widened her eyes. "A circus! That's it! We'll have a circus for Mr. Trainer's guests!"

The idea blossomed. There was room under the "big top" for all their gifts and talents. Singing. Dancing. Playing. Reciting. And acrobatics, too. The girls shouted out ideas faster than Alvin could scribble them down. Mr. Trainer's chickens scampered about, clucking at all the commotion.

At length, Alvin read aloud the draft of their circus plans. It was so lengthy on paper that they included an intermission.

"Intermission. The band plays again. That's us," said Alvin's youngest sister, taking Alvin's neatly printed list. "Then it's Dancing Girls and One Swinging One. That's you, Ida. You're best at it."

"I can walk a beam, too," said Ida, eager to try it. "And do handsprings."

"On a beam?" Alvin shuddered.

Ida giggled. "No. Not yet. But maybe someday."

Ida and her friends held a rehearsal after school the next day. It went very well, except for Three-Foot Grump. She butted Mr. Trainer's chickens, and refused to bow.

"You're a grump. All three feet of you," Alvin scolded, and took her home.

"Does your mom want to come to the dress rehearsal in the morning?" Alvin asked when he returned.

"I haven't told her yet," admitted Ida.

"Why not?"

"I'm just going to let it be a surprise," said Ida.

Alvin thought that was a good plan. Ida was unsure how she would get everyone to the carriage house after dinner the next night. But it was a minor problem in the scheme of things.

Chapter Twenty-five

As the sun sank on Saturday evening, Mr. Trainer sent Vic to pick up a distant cousin, the daughter of a past governor. He had planned to go himself, but Mom had a crisis on her hands and couldn't spare him. Dessert had boiled over in the oven. A burnt-cherry stench was seeping through the house even as the earliest guest climbed the veranda steps.

The twitch in Mom's face betrayed her frayed nerves. She told Ida to help the hired girls throw the windows open while she detoured guests from the front veranda to the rose garden, where Mr. Trainer was deployed to occupy them with a tour of the roses.

It was clear even to Aunt Lizzy, who had come to help, that the breeze would not blow the air clean in the short amount of time it took to see a few rosebushes. She dispatched the serving girls to the garden with mulled cider for the guests.

Ida had a better solution. She slipped out to the carriage house, where Alvin, his sisters, and the menagerie waited.

"Show time!" she cried.

"But they haven't even eaten yet," said Alvin.

Quickly, Ida explained Mom's dilemma.

"Who's going to bring the guests?" asked Alvin's youngest sister.

"You are," said Ida in a flash of inspiration. "All five of you. Take your instruments to the garden, and lead them back, playing a tune."

The girls were garbed in the filmy pink gowns designed for their sisters' wedding. They looked liked princesses. Who could resist such charm and beauty?

Not Alvin's parents, who were among the invited guests. They had never missed a musical recital or any other opportunity to see their children perform.

Ida and Alvin flung the carriage doors wide open to let in the waning light. The grown-ups trailed the band of fairy princesses across the dewy grass. The men spread their jackets on the dusty planks the children had erected as seating inside the carriage house. Smiling dotingly, the ladies sat down. Ida saw them cuing their husbands to join them on the applause as the music faded. Mr. Trainer didn't get a nudge because Mom wasn't with him.

Ida looked twice to be sure. She was either checking on the smoke situation or awaiting more guests. Ah, well. The show must go on. And so it did.

Mandy the singing cat was the opening act. She was supposed to sing in accompaniment with Alvin's flute-playing sister. She chose instead to growl throughout a second sister's recital of "The Goblins'll Git Ya If Ya Don't Watch Out!" It was most effective.

Alvin was in the limelight for the next few acts. First, he put Swisher through all his paces. Then he put

Mandy the cat aboard Pretty Boy Pony, and trotted them around the ring to a polite spatter of applause. Next, Three-Foot Grump took a bow, cooperating to a degree that surprised even Alvin. Alvin wrapped up the animal act with a game of toss and fetch with his crow, Tory. Tory retrieved a skate key, a coin, and a cuff link. As a grand and unplanned finale, Tory attempted to retrieve a gaudy bauble from a lady's hat.

Alvin intervened and put Tory in the chicken coop while the girls played another tune. Mr. Trainer's chickens wandered in toward the end of their selection. It was their habit, at dusk, to file into their coop within the carriage house. But they were closed out because of Tory. They circled and clucked in a quarrelsome confusion.

"Let's hear it for the Fowl Dance," said Alvin, capitalizing on their behavior.

The audience clapped. The band curtsied. The chickens darted this way and that, shedding feathers and making a general nuisance of themselves.

"I think I'm getting insight into the recent decline in egg production," said Mr. Trainer. But he smiled when he said it and did not intervene.

Ida took her mark in the ring. Alvin climbed to the loft and tossed her the looped end of the rope. His sisters scaled the loft ladder and prepared to tow Ida into position.

"And now the dainty, delightful, daring Ida Louisa will ascend to the skies on her magic swing!" Alvin's voice rang out over the carriage house.

Goose bumps danced over Ida like air bubbles as the

girls began pulling on the rope, lifting her until she was even with the floor of the loft. She had improved on her act, and planned to do a few minutes of pretty poses before the girls jumped from the loft. It would be a stunning sight, all five of them in their gossamer gowns, floating down like butterflies.

As Ida prepared to drop and hang by her knees in the loop swing, Mr. Trainer's motorcar swung up the carriage house drive with Vic at the wheel. Ida squinted in the light of the headlamps. The guests were looking, too, curious about who had arrived.

Ida hadn't waited all this time to share the show. She wanted all eyes on her. But as she delayed her knee-drop, Three-Foot Grump, whom Alvin had neglected to secure, ran at a hen.

"Get him, Daddy," said one of Alvin's sisters.

Alvin's father jumped up to herd the goat out of the carriage house. Mr. Trainer tried to help. He made a grab for the goat's lead rope. But Three-Foot was a cagey old goat. She trotted in circles below Ida, evading her captors.

"She likes to tease the chickens. Put 'em away and she'll quit," Ida offered helpfully.

Mr. Trainer let the crow out and shooed the chickens into the coop. The hens were grateful. Three-Foot was not.

"Alvin, get down here and do something with this goat," ordered Alvin's father.

But before Alvin could comply, Three-Foot caught sight of the guest getting out of the passenger's side of the motorcar. A feathered boa adorned her sparkly dress. It floated on the evening breeze.

"Grab her!" warned Alvin as Three-Foot pawed the earth and lowered her head.

Alvin's dad lunged and missed. Mr. Trainer, in an act of folly and raw courage, planted himself, a human wall between his feathered guest and Three-Foot. Alvin, the hater of heights, grabbed the rope. Startled, his sisters held on for the ride as he propelled them all out of the loft. They swung down. Ida swung up. The girls, unprepared, toppled, but clung fast to the rope.

Making the best of it, Ida, just inches from the rafters, arched her legs prettily, curled her toes, and raised one arm in a "ta-da" pose. But the act that she had practiced to be a show of grace of comeliness took an alarming twist as Alvin let go of the rope to jump for the goat. He missed, but caught Three-Foot's tail. Three-Foot bleated and turned on a dime and charged Alvin and his sisters. The sisters, well versed in goat-dodging, let go of the rope and scattered like marbles.

As if in slow motion, Ida felt every inch of her fall. She saw the audience leap to their feet. Sorted Mom's scream from a chorus of cries; saw her freeze just inside the carriage house door, her hands framing her horror-stricken face; and in the same heartbeat saw Mr. Trainer diving for the rope. It was like a writhing snake, rising to strike.

Mr. Trainer caught the tail of it with his bare hands with only inches to spare. The momentum of Ida's weight, coming down, seared his hands and knocked him off his feet. But he hung on tight. Ida landed with just slightly more grace than Alvin, who flung himself on Three-Foot's back and got bucked off.

The goat and the guests went their separate ways, posthaste. By the time Three-Foot was under lock and key, Mr. Trainer's guests had convened in the dining room. Aunt Lizzy served them the first course, while, in the kitchen, Mom sniffed and wiped her eyes and medicated Mr. Trainer's rope-burned hands.

Ida cried, too, and apologized.

"Stop that sniffling. I'm fine," insisted Mr. Trainer as Mom painted his palms with medicine that couldn't disinfect without stinging.

Seeing him wince, Ida winced, too, and blew on his hands. "Thanks for saving me," she said.

"You're welcome," he replied. "But let's have no more circus games. All right?"

As grateful as she was, Ida wouldn't make a promise she knew she couldn't keep.

Mr. Trainer lost his bid for mayor, and Alvin had to part with his goat. But, like Ida, neither of them was a quitter. Alvin replaced the goat with a rabbit he named Sneeze, and Mr. Trainer vowed to run again.

Winter came and went, and then spring, with more circus antics, which Mr. Trainer conveniently forgot he had forbidden. He even came to the first matinee in place of Mom, who sent her regrets from the upstairs bedroom window. She hadn't felt well all day.

Late in the show, as Ida was doing a one-armed swing from a swivel rigging General had helped her make, there came wafting from the same window the lusty wail of a newborn baby.

A baby sister for Ida! Ida hadn't known she wanted one until the little red fist closed around her finger. She argued long and hard for the name Sylvia in memory of Slick, whose given name was Sylvester.

Vic scoffed. Mom said absolutely not. No child of hers was being named for a runaway boy. Mr. Trainer suggested Genevieve. Ida promptly shortened it to Jennie, in memory of Jennie Ward.

Watching Jennie grow, Ida grew, too. There was so much to share with her little sister before she went away in pursuit of her circus dreams.

By the time Father was elected mayor, Ida was in high school, busy with music lessons and gymnastics and dance. And too grown up for backyard circuses. But that was not to say her dream had died. It had not. What she did in the carriage house was not play. It was hard work putting muscle on her frame, calluses on her hands, and grit in her craw.

Her dream grew with every show that came to town, every winter performance of the YMCA Circus, and every newspaper report of aspiring aerialists flocking to Bloomington for Eddie and Mayme Ward's flying school.

Florida Louisa Young was in the right place waiting for the right time. That time came, just days after her high school graduation.

Chapter Twenty-six

Sunlight crept through the windows of the barn. It shone on the cotton-stuffed rope aerialists call a "web." Ida waited until she heard the barn door open. Then, with calculated deliberation, she powdered her hands and scaled the web.

Suspended high above the floor, Ida reached for a second rope that hung from the rigging. She tucked her wrist through the loop on the end and, with a drumroll in her head, gathered strength. Then, in a union of muscle, skill, and determination, she propelled her body up and over her right shoulder. Up and over. Up and over. Up and over. Her taut, trim body whirled like a windmill. Five, six, seven, eight, nine, ten, twenty, swing-overs.

Then, back to the web and down, and up again, this time by ladder to the pedestal board and the trapeze. And there she was at long last, perched on the flying bar in Eddie Ward's practice barn.

"Hey! What do you think you're doin', kid?"

Ida's heart jumped. But this was her carefully crafted moment. The one she'd waited and practiced and planned for all her life. The bark in Eddie Ward's voice wasn't going to stop her.

"Good morning, Mr. Ward," she called down to the muscular fellow scowling up at her from the dirt floor below. "I'm Ida Lou Young. General's Useful's friend? You said to come see you when I was ready to join out. I'm ready."

"How old are you?" he growled.

"Seventeen."

"Who's your folks?"

"Herman and Anna Trainer."

"Good godfrey. You're the mayor's daughter?"

"Yes, sir," said Ida.

"Does he know you're here?"

"Yes."

"And he doesn't care?"

"He cares quite a lot," Ida replied. "He says he'll disown me."

Mr. Ward's mouth jerked, but the grin was gone before it fully formed. "That didn't change your mind?"

"No," said Ida.

"Why the blazes not?"

"Because he and Mom didn't raise me to be a quitter," said Ida.

Eddie shifted his feet and rubbed the back of his neck. Ida's pulse ticktocked in her eardrums, her dream hanging in the balance.

"Herman Trainer's daughter," he muttered. "I ought to send you home off the toe of my mules."

"He won't really disown me, Mr. Ward. He's bluffing."

Eddie glowered and held up a hand for silence. He squinted at her a long moment. "Think you can lift me?"

"Lift you?"

"If you're going to fly, you've got to catch first. Hang by your knees, and drop your arms. If you can lift me, we'll talk."

He slipped out of his mules—the shoes he wore over his practice togs—scaled the rope, and stretched his hands to Ida.

Florida Louisa, the flying girl, was on her way!

Epilogue

"And she was," Gram Jennie said, finishing her mending and her story.

"What about her dad?" asked Lacey, swinging her feet. "Did he ever come back?"

"Ida met him once in Billings, Montana. He asked to see her after the show. It had been many years. Ida didn't recognize him at first."

"But he knew her?"

"Oh, my, yes! Ida was a big star, traveling the world by then. Her image was all over the circus bills: Flying Florida Louisa Young!"

"Was Auntie Ida glad to see him?" asked Lacey.

"She was ready for him, let's put it that way," said Gram, snipping the last thread. "At first she wanted to cut him the way he had cut her by his abandonment. But as he twisted his hat and shuffled his feet and looked at her like he couldn't believe he had had any part in who she was—"

"He hadn't," Lacey broke in.

"Oh, but he had," said Gram. "By his absence, he had had a part in shaping her."

"A bad part!"

"A teaching part," said Gram. "Ida saw a little of Vic in him, and something of General, too. Not in looks; in circumstances—General had failed his first family, you'll remember. Ida knew how much he regretted that. So she gave her father the gift General had never asked of his own family, and that was a second chance."

"Did he take it?" asked Lacey.

"Not for long," said Gram.

"Poor Auntie Ida."

"She didn't feel that way. Forgiving him had freed her of all those past hurts. Anyway, she had General. And Mr. Trainer. And Vic. And her husband."

"Who did she marry?" asked Lacey.

Gram's eyes twinkled. "A young lion tamer named Alvin."

"The neighbor boy?" cried Lacey. "I didn't know that!"

"Alvin died before you were born," said Gram. "But he and Ida enjoyed many happy years together, traveling with the circus."

"What about Slick? Did Auntie Ida ever learn what became of him?"

Gram's mouth turned down. "No. She never did."

"Maybe he got out of the circus business."

"Maybe." Gram checked her watch, patted Lacey's knee, and rose from the glider. "They should be home anytime now. I'll put on the teakettle and take some cookies out of the freezer."

Lacey tumbled into the leaves onto her back. She gazed through crimson branches, wondering what sort of fabric she should use for Aunt Ida's sunbonnet girl. Something shiny and slick and glittery, like the circus.

That would make twenty-five squares for her quilt. An uneven number. Unless she included Vic. What about Mr. Trainer? He was Gram Jennie's dad—he certainly belonged.

The neighbor's beagle whined and ambled across the yard to greet her. Lacey patted his head and reached for her book. "Lie down, Sam, and I'll read to you."

Sam was old. Lying down was what he did best.

Crisp leaves crunched as Lacey rolled over on her tummy. She bent her knees and crossed her ankles. Old Sam rested his head on his paws and watched her turn pages. He dozed off just as the family van turned up the driveway.

Lacey's pulse jumped. She saw the girls unstrapping the infant seat while Dad helped Judith out of the car. "What do you think, Lace?" he called to her.

Lacey trotted over for her first look at her brother. His face was tiny and red. He pressed his fist to his puckered mouth and let out a thin wail.

"Hungry already?" cooed Judith.

"I'll feed him," cried Sheri. "Let me! Let me!"

"I'll help!" Ivana stepped out of the car, juggling cans of formula and a box of diapers.

Judith started to follow them inside. But Dad said, "Relax, honey. I'm an old hand at this. I'll show the girls the ropes while you take a breather."

Lacey thought Judith would insist on giving the baby his bottle. But she turned and plucked a leaf from Lacey's shoulder instead. "It's good to be home," she said, and kissed her hair. "You smell like Sam."

"And leaves," said Lacey, cupping her hands to her nose. "I missed you."

"Me, too," murmured Judith. Her eyes turned glassy. She caught tears with the back of her hand. "Forgive me. I don't know where they came from."

Lacey wanted to say that she cried sometimes, too, and didn't know why. But the words stuck behind the knot in her throat.

"It was hectic at the hospital. I thought we'd never get home," said Judith, drying her eyes. "Let's sit down a minute, shall we?"

Lacey slipped into the glider beside her. They held hands and admired the leaves and caught up on the news. Gram joined them there with tea and cookies and reassurances that Dad and the girls were managing nicely.

After a while, Sheri burst out the front door. "Anybody seen my basketball?"

"It's in the front closet," Gram replied.

"I looked there."

"Try the clothes hamper. I know I saw it somewhere," said Gram.

"Home, sweet, home," said Judith. She came to her feet, helped Gram gather tea things, and led the way in.

Ivana was playing "Rock-a-Bye-Baby" on the piano. She lifted a hand from the keys and touched a finger to her lips. The baby was in the cradle Gram had passed down from Dad's earliest days.

Lacey leaned over her sleeping brother. What little hair he had was as fair as pillow feathers. It begged to be touched.

"Go ahead, you won't wake him," said Judith as Lacey's hand hovered over his little head.

"In his picture he looked bald, but he isn't," whispered Lacey.

"Just fair," said Judith, smiling.

Lacey touched strands as light and soft as the fiberfill Gram used in her quilts. She stroked his tiny fingers. His fist opened. He caught her finger in his hand and held on tight.

"He's got me." Awestruck, Lacey looked from Gram to Dad to Judith. "He's holding on! He's so strong. Look at his eyebrows. They're like little sprouts."

"He's a wonder, all right," said Dad. He draped an arm over her shoulder. "Aren't you going to hold him?"

"How do I . . . I don't know how to pick him up," admitted Lacey.

Judith lifted him from the cradle and laid him gently in Lacey's arms. So tiny and helpless, still clinging to her finger. Dad nudged the rocking chair her way. She eased into it, and surprised a burp from the baby. Dad laughed. Even Gram giggled. A warm-bath feeling flooded Lacey. He fit so perfectly into her arms! She rocked and nestled and hummed and hugged.

The music stopped. Ivana slipped into the room with Sheri at her heels.

"His initials spell 'guest,' did you know?" said Ivana.

"Cool!" chimed Sheri.

"But he'll never be a guest here," said Gram, smiling. "He's come home."

"It's too much name," said Lacey. "Call him Gilly."

You're our little Gilly. Yes," she crooned, and kissed his small fist.

The girls perched on the rocking chair arms, hovering and cooing.

"What a picture," said Dad. He grinned and reached for the camera.

It flashed in Lacey's eyes, capturing a stitch in time.

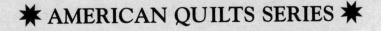

✴ AMERICAN QUILTS SERIES ✴

Activity Pages by Stasia Kehoe

BOOK 4: IDA LOU'S STORY

Make a Memory: Circus Wall

Ida Lou loves the circus. In fact, she decorates a wall in her family's tumbledown apartment with pictures of the circus and of her favorite circus performers. You can make your own picture "wall" with your favorite art form, activity, or animal as its theme. You will need:

> *A large (about 3"x 3") sheet of*
> *Fome-Cor or poster board*
> *Old newspapers, magazines, catalogs,*
> *or other printed materials*
> *Scissors*
> *A glue stick*

To begin your wall, cut out your favorite theme-related pictures from the newspapers and magazines. Using the glue stick, carefully glue the pictures onto the Fome-Cor or poster board. Allow the edges of the pictures to over-lap to create a collage effect. You may want to add pho-tographs, souvenirs (such as small posters or brochures), or captions made by cutting words from newspaper arti-cles. Do not rush to finish your wall. It make take you weeks or longer to collect the very best images for your wall. Leave space to add new material when you find it. Ask an adult to help you find the perfect spot to hang or display your special theme "wall."

Quilting Corner: Crazy Quilt Pillow

Ida Lou's first circus costume was pieced together using bits of material given to her by other circus performers. You can make a "crazy quilt" pillow with two 16" squares of felt, some fabric glue, and some scraps of unwanted material (ask parents, neighbors, or friends for scraps). Use pinking shears (or regular scissors) to cut your fabric scraps into pieces of different shapes and sizes. Arrange the cut scraps on top of one felt square, leaving a 1" margin between the edge of the felt and your pat-tern. Use fabric glue to attach the scraps to the felt, carefully gluing down one piece at a time. Leaving a 1" margin around the edge, draw an outline of glue around three sides of the second felt square. Press your crazy quilt felt (design side up) on top. When the glue has dried, stuff with polyester fiberfill or cotton balls through the fourth, unsealed, side to make a firm pillow. Glue or stitch the fourth side closed. If desired, trim edges with pinking shears or glue on a decorative strip of ribbon or lace to complete your crazy quilt pillow.

School Stories: Leaving School to Earn

In the past, children leaving school at an early age to help out with the family business or to add to the family income was not an unusual story. Imagine that it is 1918. Your mother has asked you to stop going to school and instead to go to work at a local factory. Write a short journal entry describing how this news makes you feel, whether you will try to get back to school or not, and what you imagine your future will now be like.

Family Tree Time: Fascinating Folks

In *Ida Lou's Story*, Lacey learns about the birth of her own great-grandmother and about her great-grandmother's amazing half sister. Is there a fascinating or famous person in your family tree? Ask an older relative to tell you about your most interesting ancestor. Learn more about him or her, then draw a scaled-down family tree connecting this ancestor to you.

Presenting the Past: Circus in America

The circus plays a grand role in America's past. Before movies and television, the arrival of the circus was an exciting and much-anticipated entertainment. Go to your local library or on-line to learn more about the history of the circus in America, circus parades, famous circuses and circus families, clowns and classic circus acts.

American Quilt Questions: Accepting New Family Members

Ida Lou has a difficult time accepting her mother's new relationship with Mr. Trainer, just as Lacey is struggling to accept her new stepmother and stepsisters, and getting used to the idea of a new baby joining the family.

When the story begins, what does Ida Lou think about her father's absence? Does she hope he will return? Why do you think she feels this way?

Who are some of the people who help Ida Lou's family get by in hard times? Why are these people special to Ida?

What does Ida Lou think of Mr. Trainer when she first meets him? How does she feel as she begins to realize that he is interested in marrying her mother? Why do you think Ida feels this way?

How does Mr. Trainer show Ida Lou he cares about her—before and after the accident? Does Ida Lou realize what he is trying to show her? If you were giving Ida Lou advice about getting along with her new stepfather, what would you tell her?

Does the new baby change Ida Lou's feelings about Mr. Trainer? What else might have slowly helped to change her feelings toward her stepfather?

How does Lacey feel about baby Gilly? What do you think is going to happen to Lacey and her new family? Do you think things will keep changing for the better? If you were to make a quilt for Lacey's new family, what would you call it?